Building Bridges
parental involvement in schools

Building Bridges
parental involvement in schools

Sandra Jowett and Mary Baginsky
with Morag MacDonald MacNeil

NFER-NELSON

Published by The NFER-NELSON Publishing Company Ltd,
Darville House, 2 Oxford Road East,
Windsor, Berkshire SL4 1DF, England.

First published 1991
© Crown Copyright 1991. Published by permission of the Controller of
Her Majesty's Stationery Office.

British Library Cataloguing in Publication Data
Jowett, Sandra
  Building bridges: parental involvement in schools.
  1. Great Britain
  I. Baginsky, Mary II. MacNeil, Morag MacDonald
  371.103

  ISBN 0-7005-1261-6
  ISBN 0-7005-1262-4 Pbk

Phototypeset by David John Services Ltd, Maidenhead, Berkshire
Printed by Billings & Sons Ltd, Worcester

ISBN 0 7005 1261 6 (Hardback)
Code 8343 02 4

ISBN 0 7005 1262 4 (Paperback)
Code 8344 02 4

Contents

Foreword

How best to bring up children so as to enable them to make the maximum use of their talents is a vexed question. Early on, controversies over feeding, sleeping and crying behaviours are common. At a later stage – when children are in school – there are controversies over the best way to teach reading and whether the school climate is too repressive or too permissive.

Few appear to doubt, however, the value of close parent–school collaboration. Indeed, recent legislation has sought to increase the powers of parents within the educational system. For individual children, the benefits of the home and the school sharing the same values, being in broad agreement on the best approaches and assisting each other in their endeavours, are obvious. Research findings from the USA, the Bristol longitudinal study and from the ILEA study of junior schools have confirmed the early work of both Jack and Barbara Tizard and emphasized the importance of parental involvement in children's schooling.

Despite this knowledge about its importance, very little is known about the number and variety of initiatives to increase parental involvement being pursued by schools in England and Wales. It was in order to fill this gap that the Department of Education and Science, in 1986, commissioned the National Foundation for Educational Research to carry out a large-scale research project. The aims and methods adopted by the Research Team and the principal findings, and the implications of these findings for all those involved with children's schooling, form the content of this book.

As chairman of the Project Steering Committee, I wish to record my thanks to the Department of Education and Science for their support. I also wish to thank the members of the Committee for the time and energy that they have committed to the Project. Finally, I wish to pay tribute to Sandra Jowett and the members of the Research Team. The research was complex and required sensitive methods, and frequently entailed arduous field study.

The team responded to these challenges with both enthusiasm and dedication. This book is a fitting record of that work. It should be of value to school governors charged with the task of ensuring that schools are responsive to parent and pupil needs, heads and teachers striving to make their schools more open, local education authority officers and advisers responsible for policy formulation, and to all those involved in the education service – as professionals or as parents – who appreciate the value of parental involvement in children's schooling and wish to increase its scope and efficacy.

Peter Mortimore
Deputy Director
Institute of Education
University of London

Acknowledgements

This research could not have been undertaken without the active collaboration of a large number of people whom we would like to thank for their generous cooperation and support. This includes the many teachers and other staff in the local education authorities who participated in this study. We are also grateful to the parents who talked so fully about their experiences. These interviews, and those with the pupils, formed the backbone of our study and we appreciated the time and thought given to our requests for information. Thanks are also due to the chief education officers/directors of education, advisers, inspectors and headteachers who completed our questionnaires.

We are most grateful for the advice and support received from members of the Steering Committee. They gave considerable thought to our work throughout its three-year duration, and Peter Mortimore chaired the Committee in a way that maximized the benefits we gained from their insights and suggestions.

Judy Bradley, as project director, supported the team's work throughout. Warm thanks are extended to her and to our colleagues, Wendy Keys and Joanna Le Metais, who read an earlier draft of the report and gave constructive advice.

Maura Williams-Stock was the project secretary who conscientiously dealt with many administrative tasks, as well as bearing major responsibility for the typing of the report; Moci Carter's assistance with the typing was much appreciated, and we would like to thank them both for their efficiency and patience. The assistance provided by the NFER library staff was valued.

We are grateful to the Department of Education and Science for funding this study.

Steering Committee

Peter Mortimore (Chair)	Institute of Education, University of London.
Gerry Bailey	Community Education Development Centre.
Nick Cornwell	Department of Education and Science.
John Davis	Liverpool Education Authority.
John Evans	Headteacher.
Ian Hughes	Department of Education and Science.
Barbara Megson	Her Majesty's Inspectorate.
Gillian Pugh	National Children's Bureau.
Shirley Wright	Parent.

The National Foundation for Educational Research

The National Foundation for Educational Research in England and Wales was founded in 1946 and is Britain's leading educational research institution. It is an independent body undertaking research and development projects on issues of current interest in all sectors of the public educational system. Its membership includes all the local education authorities in England and Wales, the main teachers' associations, and a large number of other major organizations with educational interests.

Its approach is scientific, apolitical and non-partisan. By means of research projects and extensive field surveys it has provided objective evidence on important educational issues for the use of teachers, administrators, parents and the research community. The expert and experienced staff that has been built up over the years enables the Foundation to make use of a wide range of modern research techniques, and, in addition to its own work, it undertakes a large number of specially sponsored projects at the request of government departments and other agencies.

The major part of the research programme relates to the maintained educational sector – primary, secondary and further education. A further significant element has to do specifically with local education authorities and training institutions. The current programme includes work on the education of pupils with special needs, monitoring of pupil performance, staff development, national evaluation and major curriculum programmes, test development, and information technology in schools. The Foundation is also the national agency for a number of international research and information exchange networks.

The NFER-NELSON Publishing Company are the main publishers of the Foundation's research reports. These reports are now available in the NFER *Research Library*, a collection that provides the educational community with up-to-date research into a wide variety of subject areas. In addition, the Foundation and NFER-NELSON work closely together to provide a wide range of open and closed educational tests and a test advisory service. NFER-NELSON also publish *Educational Research*, the termly journal of the Foundation.

1 Background, Aims and Methodology

Introduction

'Parental involvement' is undoubtedly one of the most important issues in the current educational debate. The basic concept is not of course new, but in recent years there have been a number of developments in attitudes, policies and practices which have attracted widespread interest. This is evident from the large, and rapidly increasing, academic literature on the topic and the frequent references to it in the media. This interest has been reflected in and fuelled by legislation. The Education Acts of 1980, 1981, 1986 and, much more significantly, 1988 all refer to some of the many aspects of the relationship between home and school such as choice of school, access to information, involvement in assessment and representation on governing bodies. As such, they have profound implications for the role of parents in the education of their children.

There is debate, and some excitement, about the potential gains to be made from developing contact between home and school. The emphasis is not only on increasing the involvement of parents in schools, but also on increasing the 'accountability' of schools to parents. The concept of 'accountability' has influenced both practice in schools in relation to parents (for example, DES, 1989) and the framing of legislation designed to provide a structure within which aspects of contact between home and schools can be enhanced. The recent legislation has introduced the National Curriculum and national testing of pupils at the ages of seven, 11, 14 and 16, which will provide a standard by which parents may measure their children's progress in relation to the learning objectives of the National Curriculum. Parents will also have access to aggregated test results from individual schools.

There are other areas in which the role of parents in relation to schools has been extended. Under the 'open enrolment' section of the 1988 Education Act, parents are now able to enrol their children in any school that has the 'physical capacity' for them. They have more representation, and potentially more influence, on school governing bodies and, in certain circumstances, they can initiate the process of a school moving from local education authority (LEA) control to centrally funded grant maintained status. Earlier legislation (Education (No. 2) Act 1986) had already given parents the opportunity to meet with their school governors each year to discuss matters relating to the school, through the requirement that an Annual Parents' Meeting should be convened, to be preceded by a written report from the governing body for parents.

The study reported here takes note of the various developments, both statutory and informal, towards this greater accountability in the education system. But its main concern is with other ways in which parents are involved in their own children's schooling. The focus is on their involvement in their children's curricular activities, on their role in transition (children starting or changing school) and on the information and support they receive from schools and services.

The scene was set more than 20 years ago when the Plowden Report (1967) stated that 'teachers are linked to parents by the children for whom they are both responsible. The triangle should be completed and a more direct relationship established between teachers and parents. They should be partners in more than name.' A decade later, the Warnock Report (1978) stated: 'The successful education of children with special educational needs is dependent on the full involvement of their parents: indeed, unless the parents are seen as equal partners in the educational process the purpose of our report will be frustrated.'

The vital role that parents can play in the intellectual development of their children has long been acknowledged (for example, Katz, 1982). The potential gains from drawing parents into the learning process have been re-emphasized in a recent study of children in infant classes (Tizard et al., 1988) which reported that, 'Parents had a big influence on the level of preschool attainments' and that 'those children with a head start tended to maintain it on the whole'. Tizard and her colleagues found that many parents were working with their children at home and wished to continue to do so, while Tizard and Hughes (1984) concluded from their study of pre-school children that, 'The home provides a very powerful learning environment', and indeed identified 'constraints on school staff which make it difficult for them to be as educationally effective as parents'.

The most frequently quoted recent literature on parental involvement is that concerned with reading, stemming from the important and influential work in Haringey, where parents were involved with their children in this aspect of the curriculum (Tizard, Schofield and Hewison, 1982). The Haringey research and that in Coventry (Widlake and Macleod, 1984) bear testimony to the powerful impact such practices can have on children's attainment.

Other pioneering parental involvement projects have been described in accounts of good practice (for example, Pugh et al., 1987a, 1987b) and serve as sources of inspiration for practitioners. The longitudinal study (over a period of more than 15 years) of young people who took part in pre-school programmes in the USA (Lazar and Darlington, 1982) concluded that the 'direct involvement of parents in intervention programmes was an important element in the children's improved functioning later on and that the provision of services for the whole family resulted in even more gains for the children'.

It is also clear that increased contact between home and school could potentially enhance the quality of provision generally and that it would be welcomed by many. Mortimore and his colleagues (1988) stated their belief that 'parents have a role to play in improving schools' and that 'one of the key factors associated with effective schools...is parental involvement'. A study of home–school links in secondary schools (Woods, 1984) found that one-quarter of parents would have liked to be more involved in school and that this varied little by social class. The author also identified some unmet demands; for example, more than two-fifths of parents would have liked an explanation of the teaching methods used, and more than one-third would have welcomed details of what was being taught.

The Elton Report (1989) focused on parental involvement as a mechanism for improving relationships between home and school, with potential benefits for children, and as a means of dealing with disruption in schools. The Committee recommended that 'parents should take full advantage of all formal and informal channels of communication made available by schools' and that 'Headteachers and teachers should develop policies to secure easy access to them by parents and good communications between them and parents, which go beyond the provision of formal parents' evenings'.

However, the need to guard against over-simplifying what is such 'involvement' emerges from some studies. An investigation of parental involvement in the nursery and infant years reported that many parents were eager to know about their children's learning, even if they were reluctant to enter school (Tizard, Mortimore and Burchell, 1981). In their study of secondary schools, Johnson and Ransom (1983) found that teachers tended to measure parental involvement with their children in terms of parents' visits to the school, but that parents who did not come were not necessarily apathetic and were providing many home-based forms of support that teachers were unaware of.

The study of parental involvement is complex, given the range of activities being undertaken, the differing perspectives held by participants on the desired aims and the *ad hoc* and disparate nature of much of the work. Discussions with a large number of parents, practitioners and academic staff during this research have indicated a wide diversity of opinion not only on which activities should be developed with parents, but also on the basic principles underlying this work. An activity which involves contact between home and school may be regarded as an end in itself by some, whereas others may see it primarily as a catalyst that will lead to other valuable developments. Some teachers, for example, see parental assistance with the children's activities in their schools as the goal of their work with parents. For others, such contact is only one part of a larger process which one headteacher in this study described as "parents building up a deeper understanding of school methods and teachers' understanding about home backgrounds".

Some specific schemes have been established in schools with precise aims and a clear strategy. Most initiatives, however, are much more difficult to define. One adviser said that it was extremely difficult to identify *real* involvement, but she felt that it was "something to do with meeting the needs of a whole range of parents and being very sensitive to what they wanted from the school".

There is debate about what is, and should be, the basis of parents' interest. One headteacher, for example, reported that parents of pupils in her school support the school generously in its aims and provide resources, but do not see it as appropriate to work as complementary educators with their children. Many others interviewed in this research have expressed the view that most parents are extremely interested in and wish to assist with their own children's progress but are not, and indeed, some would say, should not be, concerned with broader school issues. However, this attitude has been criticized on occasion by those who would like to broaden the base of parents' contact. The various roles that parents do (and potentially could) play are discussed throughout this report.

The research

The research presented in this report was commissioned by the Department of Education and Science (DES) for a period of three years to investigate the wide range of activities that are termed 'parental involvement' and to study a small number of them in detail. Its aims were to describe and comment critically on a wide variety of types of contact between home and school, to provide information and insights to assist those involved in developing this contact and to identify those forms of contact which were both beneficial and achievable. It is frequently assumed that parental involvement is a valuable activity per se, without any real understanding of what the phrase encompasses or of the underlying principles. The findings shed light on some of the complex issues involved in home–school relations and suggest ways in which current practice may be enhanced and developed. They will be of value to those who want to examine home–school relations in depth and to develop strategies for achieving the goals they have set.

Given the very rapid changes set in train by the 1988 Education Act, there is a real danger that parental involvement may be perceived narrowly, with the emphasis on the formal publication of information by schools and the representation of parents on governing bodies. The study reported here points the way towards developing and maintaining effective relationships with parents beyond the formal minimum.

In the initial stages of the research, preliminary visits were made to more than 100 institutions, individuals and projects to collect information about the range of work being undertaken. Such extensive visiting was necessary because of the diverse and complex nature of the topic of enquiry. Contact was also made with relevant national and local organizations and further information was obtained in response to publicity about the research in the national press. Following these preliminary soundings, the main work was undertaken in two distinct but related parts, each with its own methodology.

Information from the LEAs

Each LEA in England and Wales was sent three questionnaires enquiring about developments in work with parents in their area. The first was a short questionnaire sent to Chief Education Officers/Directors of Education, and a response rate of 91 per cent was achieved. It was designed to collect information about how LEAs were developing their work with parents, the existence of any guidelines, policy statements and other documents, and the establishment of working parties to review policies and priorities. Questions about the composition of governing bodies and other opportunities for the formal representation of parents were included.

Two further questionnaires were distributed to each LEA and most were completed by advisers/inspectors. The first was concerned with pre-school and primary education, and 78 per cent of these were returned. The second was about the secondary stage, and a response rate of 77 per cent was achieved. These questionnaires concentrated on the involvement of parents with their own children in aspects of the curriculum and more general parental involvement in schools. Details of accommodation allocated for the use of parents, training courses, specific appointments to develop parental involvement and designated community schools were also sought. Findings from these three surveys are presented in Appendix A.

The case studies

The responses to the questionnaires produced a wealth of information about initiatives currently being developed in England and Wales, and an overview of these was produced during the research (Jowett and Baginsky, 1988). The data also informed the selection of 11 schools, schemes or services for detailed investigation. These covered a wide range in terms of both the age of the children (pre-school, primary and secondary) and the type of involvement. At one end of the spectrum was a home visiting team, who worked with pre-school children with special educational needs and their parents in their homes; and at the other end was a process to involve parents in their children's subject choices for General Certificate of Secondary Education (GCSE) courses. The 11 case studies are summarized in Chapter 2, and they are described in detail in Appendix B. In selecting the places for detailed study, care was taken to ensure a geographical spread across England and Wales and that children from ethnic minority groups and from different socio-economic backgrounds were represented.

Method

The main sources of information in the case studies were semi-structured interviews conducted with parents (some of whom were seen individually, and some in couples) and staff. The majority of the parent interviews lasted for at least an hour; some were considerably longer. All the interviews took place in the parents' homes. Most of the teacher interviews lasted for approximately an hour.

Because of the nature of the investigation, significantly more parents than staff took part in this study as there were far more of the former to draw from. Very few people declined to take part in the study. For some activities, it was appropriate and realistic for all those taking part to be included in the research; but in other cases, a sample was taken. A total of 181 parent interviews were undertaken and a further 11 parents took part in discussion groups. Questionnaires were completed by 72 parents from two settings, which represented a response rate of 72 per cent. There were 87 interviews with members of staff. In one secondary school six pupils, taking part in the home–school reading initiative, were also interviewed. The numbers of parents and staff asked specific questions are given in Appendix C.

In addition to the interviews, each of the 11 places selected for detailed study was visited a number of times. Meetings of various kinds for parents were attended; home visitors were accompanied on visits; literature prepared for parents was read; and relevant background information was gathered through visits to schools and discussions with key individuals. The aim was to establish a comprehensive, all-round view of the contact being developed with parents.

Other sources of information

The questionnaires distributed to LEAs were a means of surveying the national picture and collecting general background material. The case-study work generated very detailed information about a small number of developments. To provide information of a different order between these levels, a questionnaire was distributed to more than 400 randomly selected headteachers across England and Wales. This asked about current practice with parents, and sought views on a number of related issues; a response rate of 85 per cent was achieved. Some of the findings from this questionnaire are included in Chapter 4, and the rest will be published separately.

In addition to the case studies, data were also collected from two other sources of particular interest. One secondary school had a Parents' Consultative Group which provided a forum for parents to discuss issues pertaining to school life, and these meetings were monitored. The other source was a team established in one authority specifically to develop work with parents in schools. The members of this team were interviewed. Details of these developments follow the descriptions of the schools, schemes and services in Chapter 2.

The chapters

Chapter 3 describes the wide variety of ways in which parents can be involved in the curriculum with their children by working with them at home or school, or both, and discusses some of the misunderstandings and lost opportunities that characterize this practice. Chapter 4 is concerned with meetings established in schools, both those to inform and those designed to involve parents actively in schools. Chapter 5 looks at parental involvement as children start or change school and considers some key issues in transition and the merits of various strategies. Chapter 6 presents material from parents and teachers on the subject of home visiting and gives details of some well-established schemes incorporating this practice.

The more routine day-to-day contacts, which have implications for developing policies and practice, are the focus of Chapter 7. Chapter 8 considers the practice and views of staff actively engaged in the development and execution of work with parents, and some of the pitfalls and potential gains are explored. The implications of the research findings are considered in Chapter 9, which concludes with a consideration of possible ways forward in the development of contact between parents and schools and services.

2 The Studies of Parental Involvement

Introduction

This chapter summarizes the schools, schemes and services selected for case-study work; these comprise:

- two concerned with pre-school children;
- five focusing on the primary years;
- four involving secondary schools.

In addition, information from two other sources is included:

- a parental involvement team of advisory teachers; and
- a parents' consultative group.

The descriptions provide a context for the findings presented in the remainder of the report.

For each school, scheme or service, an indication is given of the age range of the children catered for, the type of community served and the nature of the parental involvement studied. More detailed accounts are given in Appendix B, which includes information about the samples of parents and teachers chosen and the research methods used. (All names used are fictitious.)

Pre-school

Newborough LEA's Early Years Support Team — a pre-school team working with children with special educational needs
This team is part of the educational provision of a small, urban LEA, working in a socially mixed area, mostly with white families. It consists of four qualified teachers who work with

pre-school children with special educational needs and their parents at home, on an authority-wide basis.

As well as providing parents with ideas for activities and strategies to use with their children, it is hoped that the teachers will get to know the families with whom they work and be able to offer other support as required. It is a policy of the team, however, that no one teacher works with a family for more than 18 months. In this way, the children learn that they have different teachers at different times in their lives and parents are encouraged not to become dependent on one person.

An important part of the team's work is the way it involves parents in the review procedure, including the writing of reports, as the children approach school age. The intention is to place parents on equal terms with the professionals who have been involved with their children.

Dalebridge Nursery School's Family Support Project

This nursery school serves a predominantly working-class, white, urban community, where one-fifth of the pupils are of Asian origin. It has 160 children on roll, about half of whom attend in the morning and half in the afternoon, and they usually enter the nursery during their fourth year.

In the early 1980s, the school requested, and was granted, money for a Family Support Project, and as a result, an educational home visitor (EHV) was appointed. As part of her work, she visits prospective pupils and their parents at home when the child is registered for a nursery place. The visits usually last for about half an hour and provide an opportunity for the parents to hear about the school and to discuss their child and any concerns or queries they may have. In a few cases, long-term visiting is undertaken and, if the EHV is concerned about a child or if a problem is discussed during the visit, the parent and child may be invited to a pre-nursery group.

The EHV runs three such groups in the school, each involving about six parents. They are designed to provide an opportunity for children to engage in a range of activities and for parents to draw support from one another and the EHV.

Primary

Lane End Infants — a school with a range of parental involvement
This urban infant school serves a socially mixed catchment area where approximately one-quarter of the three- to seven-year-old pupils are from ethnic minority groups. Contact with parents takes a variety of forms, including a school policy advisory group, a parents' coffee area and notice board, information leaflets and a twice-termly newsletter.

This is a school where the headteacher and some members of staff see contact with parents as a priority. The school policy advisory group is composed both of parents and teachers. It looks critically and constructively at school procedures and practices, and suggests ways in which they could be developed. Parents are invited to attend school assemblies, to help in classrooms and around the school and to become involved in the Parents' Association. The information leaflets cover a wide range of topics, including reading, water and sand play, and what happens in school during lunchtime; one lists local community organizations, while another deals with child abuse.

Parents are encouraged to discuss their child's progress informally and to enquire about the school's programme of learning. They are welcome in the school at any time.

Tatehill First School — an induction programme for starting school
This school is situated in an urban area and the children come from a socially mixed community where the vast majority of people are white.

Drawing on research that documented the difficulties children experienced in starting school, an induction programme with several elements that focused on the main areas of discontinuity for children was devised by the headteacher, one reception class teacher (although it was used in both reception classes) and an educational psychologist. The intention was to extend contact with parents around the period of transition, on the assumption that this would enable parents to prepare their children more effectively for school and lay the foundations for a good parent–teacher working relationship.

The programme consists of meetings with parents – both before and after children have started school – an introductory video and a set of Starting School packs. The video was made in school and features those activities within a reception child's day that have been shown to cause most difficulty for new entrants such as lunchtime, playtime and getting ready for PE. Each pack covers one of five themes, for example, time and colour, and the intention is that each child has the opportunity to work through one pack on each theme. The materials within a pack are carefully designed to interrelate so that they reinforce the key points and skills to be learned. Each pack contains a parent–child booklet which explains to parents how the activities should be tackled, as well as the underlying rationale.

Millshire LEA's Home-School Reading Initiative
This is a fairly widespread service in a large, rural authority, available to pupils aged five to eight from a variety of social backgrounds, the vast majority of whom are white. The aim is to involve parents in their children's school activities, with an emphasis on reading.

Books and games are available for parents to share with their children at home; and some schools hold workshops for parents and children in school. Responsibility for the organization and running of the scheme lies with two primary advisers, while two advisory teachers have a substantial part of their working week allocated to it. Schools are given resources and time to support the work – and are free to develop it as they choose. They have responded in various ways, all intended to enhance parents' involvement with their own children in the curriculum.

Stanfield Middle School – a school with a policy on home visiting
This middle school has an urban setting and caters for approximately 340 pupils aged from eight to 12 years, about 95 per cent of whom are Asian. Most of the parents are engaged in manual or semi-skilled occupations.

A variety of attempts have been made by staff to improve contact with parents, after a history of very little parental involvement. Many of the parents were not educated in this country, and the headteacher is concerned to provide as much information as possible on what goes on in the school, as well as being particularly anxious to show parents that their culture is also valued. Home visits are made to first-year pupils to discuss the importance of reading with children and to encourage parents to come into school. In addition, a video detailing the school's approach to reading is available to parents.

The school leaflet states that parents are welcome in school, at any time, and that more formal open meetings take place each term. Curriculum evenings are also held to give parents information about what is done in school.

Planeborough LEA's Working with Parents Team
Planeborough is an urban authority that includes both industrial, working-class areas and a middle-class commuter belt. It has an ethnically mixed population. An authority-wide team was set up three years ago to help schools catering for pupils aged three to 12 years to develop their work. It consists of four teachers seconded to the scheme one day a week for a year.

Three key areas are addressed: home–school liaison, including home visiting, developing induction courses for new parents and improving communication between home and school; improvement of parent and toddler clubs by providing a broader range of activities; and developing courses for parents to inform them of what the schools are trying to do and to stress the value of cooperation between parents and teachers.

The work which has been supported in schools is very varied. The basic objectives, however, have always been that schools should work towards their own whole-school policy of parents as partners and that the expertise which is developed in this area should be shared with teachers in other schools as much as possible.

Secondary

The Home–School Liaison Committee at Woodvale Comprehensive
Woodvale is a mixed, 11–18 comprehensive community school serving a mainly working-class, white population in an urban setting.

The Home–School Liaison Committee comprises four parents from each year – elected or re-elected annually – the parent governors, the headteacher and four other members of staff. It meets termly and provides an opportunity for parents and staff to discuss general school matters and policy. The idea evolved in response to concern about the low level of interest in the previous Parent–Teacher Association. Staff attend on a voluntary basis.

In addition to the Home–School Liaison Committee, there are home–school groups for years one to five in the school. These meet twice termly – once to discuss the reports that are produced on each pupil, and once to discuss wider educational issues. The discussion meetings attract between eight and ten per cent of parents and reports on each are presented to the Home–School Liaison Committee by parent representatives from each year group.

Banthorpe Comprehensive School's transition programme for first-year pupils
This school is mixed and caters for nearly 800 pupils aged between 11 and 16 in a socially mixed, white, rural community.

The transition programme has been designed to ease the transfer to secondary school and consists of a variety of meetings for parents and pupils. The aims are to increase parents' understanding of the curriculum and teaching methods used, and to demonstrate to children that parents and teachers work together with the pupils' interests in mind. It is hoped that parents will become well known to the form tutors and have the opportunity to express their views on any aspect of school life.

In this school, the approach to dealing with children's transfer to secondary school is being developed by one head of department, building on some existing practice. He is enthusiastic and keen to motivate colleagues. During a recent one-year secondment, he had the opportunity to clarify his aims, and the induction programme grew out of that.

Marksbury Community School – a secondary school with parental involvement in GCSE options
Marksbury is a mixed comprehensive school catering for 11- to 18-year-olds. It is located at the edge of a city, and the catchment area is predominantly working class with approximately one-third of pupils from ethnic minority groups. The school was recently designated a community college and school.

As part of a developing policy of contact with parents, the school has devised a series of meetings and related booklets on GCSE options, designed to inform parents of, and involve them in, the decisions which face their children.

The first booklet is sent home with pupils towards the end of October in their third year in the school, together with a letter inviting parents to a meeting in early November. The second booklet – which contains more detailed information on subjects

— is distributed shortly after this event. Parents are then invited to a consultation evening with individual subject teachers at the end of November to discuss children's progress in specific subjects with particular reference to the GCSE course and options. At the beginning of March, parents are again invited into the school to meet tutors to discuss the choices which have been made by their children. It is expected that the completed forms indicating individual subjects will have been returned before this meeting, so that decisions can be finalized on that evening.

Overlea Community Comprehensive School — contact with parents around the time of transition, a home–school reading project and local authority support
This school is situated in a small town in a rural area. It serves a white, socially mixed community, and has approximately 630 pupils aged between 11 and 16.

Overlea has an induction programme for pupils starting school that consists of meetings for them and their parents. It also has a home–school reading project for first-year pupils experiencing difficulty with their reading. An essential ingredient of this work is a visit made to the homes of all the children taking part.

The two strands of contact between home and school came about because of the commitment of individual members of staff to certain aims. Both developments received extra impetus from an LEA initiative to promote the idea of 'parents as partners'. As part of this project, Overlea was granted a substantial number of supply days to provide replacement teachers for those staff engaged in work with parents. The advisory headteacher attached to the school as part of the LEA scheme also offered to help in any appropriate way and provided school-based in-service training.

Other sources of information

The Parental Involvement Team in Stileborough — a team of advisory teachers who support schools to work with parents
This is an example of a permanent group of teachers, funded specifically to work with colleagues in schools and parents to develop a variety of activities. It was established five years ago in a small, urban authority which has a high proportion of Asian families and several densely populated housing-estates. It was originally intended that the team's work would span the

three to 16 years age group, but many people assumed that it was confined to the early-years sector (partly because the adviser involved also has responsibility for early-years education), and it is proving difficult to move up through the age range.

The project is directed by an adviser, and the team consists of three advisory teachers and a nursery nurse. They work in schools across the authority to encourage parents to become involved as the educators of their own children; to promote a partnership between home and school; and to foster a welcoming atmosphere in schools. They undertake a variety of activities, including organizing parents' groups where aspects of the curriculum are explained and discussed; working in classrooms with parents and children; and home visiting. They also provide in-service training for teachers in the authority.

The Parents' Consultative Group at Pendinge Comprehensive School
Pendinge is a comprehensive school situated in a rural location and drawing pupils from a town and several outlying villages. It serves a socially mixed, white catchment area.

The Parents' Consultative Group was established in the school when the recently appointed headteacher took up his post. It meets about once a month, and as the prospectus states, 'everyone is welcome'. It is hoped that a minimum of two parents from each year group in the school will be present. Between 25 and 45 parents attend the meetings, which are designed as a forum for discussing and reviewing the work of each year group, on the understanding that the headteacher will follow up any queries or concerns before the next meeting.

3 Parental Involvement in the Curriculum with Their Own Children

Introduction

One phrase that regularly appears in books and articles on parental involvement describes parents as 'complementary educators' who work directly with their children in ways that reinforce or extend what is being undertaken in school. In this research, parents and teachers were asked about this type of contact between home and school. Both groups were asked for their views on parents going into school specifically to work with their own children. The parents and teachers of pre-nursery and primary-age children were asked for their views on parental involvement in children's reading. Questions about 'activities to continue at home' and 'guidance about things for parents to do with their children' were put to the parents and teachers of young children, while those concerned with secondary-age pupils were asked about homework.

As well as reporting on the responses to these questions, this chapter also contains findings from three of the places selected for detailed study. One is the home–school initiative in Overlea Comprehensive School for first-year pupils who were identified as having difficulty with reading. Another is Millshire's scheme where parents were invited by primary schools to participate with their children in a range of activities, mostly related to the development of reading. The views of parents and teachers on the workshops held in some schools are reported here. The third study is of the ways in which parents were involved with their children in the process of choosing GCSE options in Marksbury Comprehensive School.

Parents working with their own children in school

The parents from Millshire were the only ones who had experience of going into school regularly, specifically to work with their own children, and most of them thought it a good idea. In the other case-study schools, the number of parents who would welcome this form of contact varied from none at all to nearly half of them.

Among parents who were positive about this arrangement, the most common response was that going into school would give an insight into what pupils were doing. As one mother said: "They could explain to me what he was doing and I would be able to tackle it better at home. It would be good for him to have that individual attention."

The reasons given for lack of enthusiasm for the idea were that children would behave inappropriately with their parents around and that teaching should be left to the professionals who were experienced and able to achieve more with the children concerned. As one of them explained: "She would do more for her teacher than for me when it comes to lessons. She'd say she was fed-up, whereas the teacher would have the authority."

The two teachers in the special needs department of Overlea Comprehensive had run a few sessions where parents had come in to work with their own children and they were keen to further develop this work. Staff working in the home–school reading initiative in Millshire, who were running weekly workshops, saw them as valuable additions to their home–school work with benefits for all concerned. In the other case-study schools and schemes, teachers without this experience had reservations about how children would behave and were concerned about those whose parents could not, or would not, come. A general response was illustrated by the teacher who said that the situation would be "artificial" and the "children wouldn't know who was in charge".

It is of interest that staff in the two situations where parents had had this opportunity were very enthusiastic about this form of contact and did not voice the same concerns as their colleagues who had not had this experience.

Reading at home and at school

In many families reading with children was said to be a regular activity and there were parents who had shared books with their children since babyhood. In Lane End Infants School, for example, nearly half the parents said that they read at least daily to their children, nearly one-quarter at least weekly and a few sometimes. There were only five parents from this school who said their children were not interested in this activity. Similarly, of the parents from Millshire who had attended the reading workshops in school, all but one said that they read to their children at home, and the one who did not explained that her daughter "reads several books a week to herself". Three-fifths of parents said that reading took place "every day" and the rest that it was "once a week or more".

Teachers' estimates of how many parents were reading with their children at home were lower than the information collected from parents would suggest. None of the primary schools had a policy of involving parents in a structured way with their child's reading. A typical comment was that parents were involved "in so much as they are encouraged to listen to their children read".

Individual teachers within the same school sometimes had different approaches to sending books home. In Lane End Infants School, for example, there were two teachers who sent home a book only when a child could easily read it, two who sent a reading scheme book or a library book each Friday and one who sent scheme books home "as often as possible". Parents were expected to adapt to such variations in practice when their children changed teachers, which they did not find a satisfactory arrangement.

The lack of an agreed policy on involving parents in reading was clearly illustrated by the nine headteachers interviewed from Planeborough. In four of their schools parents were asked to listen to their children reading at home, and two schools operated the practice referred to earlier of reading books being taken home only after they have been worked through. One headteacher explained the thinking behind this as being that "the children whose parents listen to them read get extra support, but the children who do not get this support at home do not suffer – they have done all the work on it in class". The other three schools had somewhat different approaches, with one headteacher saying she "dissuaded" parents who asked for books and another that the school would give them to parents who spontaneously asked.

Activities to continue at home

There were some very positive responses from parents to the idea of having activities to continue with their children at home. In Stanfield Middle School all of the parents interviewed were in favour of it. The parents involved in Millshire's home–school reading initiative also gave it their unanimous support. Most of the parents from Lane End Infants School felt that it would be a useful development. Other responses were less enthusiastic, the most muted coming from the group of parents whose children had just started at Tatehill First School. The majority felt that the children were too young and the school day too long for them to welcome any extra activities.

Several parents said that this development would give them useful insights into the work being covered. One mother explained that she would like "more of the day-to-day work, not just reading books, which would help the children and give us a better idea". Parents also wanted to have activities at times that were convenient to them and the child, rather than as daily 'homework'.

Dissatisfaction was expressed by some parents, both in relation to staff's resistance to their taking resources home and to the lack of appeal of resources currently available to them. Staff were not generally in favour of primary-age children taking activities home on a regular basis and did not see a role for parents in reinforcing or supplementing what was undertaken in school. There was concern about 'overloading' pupils and adversely affecting other aspects of their life if 'work' went home.

However, staff did emphasize the importance of responding to the overtures of parents, who specifically asked for activities to do. One of the headteachers from Planeborough typified the responses by saying that the school always "says 'yes' to parents if they ask if they can help at home, but begs them to see the teacher, so that they are doing the same as the teacher".

In Stanfield Middle School, where the parents were unanimously in favour of activities being taken home, the different perspectives of home and school were clear. It was school policy to give homework regularly to pupils in only the top two years, and the first-year form teachers (who were teaching the children of the parents interviewed) were not in favour of work being done at home, although they did want children to be reading regularly. One member of staff said, "We are under a lot of pressure from parents to give children homework. Our perception is that much of this pressure arises from their wish that we should keep them [the children] out of their hair." Such a perception needs clarifying to ensure that the benefits of the collaborative work that parents could undertake are not lost.

Guidance from school for parents

In Stanfield Middle School, all but two of the parents were reported as wanting to receive more guidance from staff. In the other schools, either one-half or one-third of parents wanted more guidance. It was clear that many parents were doing activities with their child at home that were similar to those undertaken at school, and that some information on how they could best spend this time would be welcomed.

Some parents from Lane End Infants School, who felt confused about how they could best help their children to learn, had asked staff what they should be doing at home and had received vague replies such as "nothing in particular". Again, most parents wanted guidance in a broad sense, rather than prescribed activities which had to be done in a set time. As one father explained, "It's not exactly guidance, but I do want to know what Barry needs training on so we could sit down and help him".

While several teachers felt that benefits would accrue from parents receiving guidance from staff, the general feeling was that parents should only be given advice if they asked for it and there was concern not to put pressure on them. In Dalebridge Nursery, for example, the headteacher felt that "we are not here to tell them what to do with their child at home", but that "we will tell them how to encourage pre-reading skills if they ask". The educational home visitor in the school was in a minority, in that she saw a more active role for the school and said that it had to be realized that "these ideas don't come out of the blue to parents" and that they "generally read all the baby [care] books, but there it stops".

Some concern about how such requests from parents were dealt with by staff was expressed. The need for a sensitive approach was emphasized by a deputy headteacher who explained that guidance given in a patronizing way could actually be harmful because, "parents internalize that they are failing". She would wholeheartedly support the "right sort of guidance" but said that "asking questions like the ones I have heard teachers ask such as, 'do you have toys for your children at home?' are just annoying and irritating".

Homework

There was a remarkable variation from parents regarding the amount of homework that was done. Of the group of third-year parents at Marksbury Comprehensive School, for example, two said that their children did between two and three hours' work each evening; four said their children did not get much homework at all; three were unsure about what their children did get; and five were 'happy' with the hour (or in one case, a half-hour) that was set. The remaining seven said that the amount set varied dramatically from evening to evening. Some parents of first-year pupils would have welcomed more homework. In Banthorpe Comprehensive School this applied to the majority, and in Overlea Comprehensive to one-half of the parents.

The general response from parents was that while they were interested in knowing that what was set had actually been done, they did not take a very active role in what was done at home. The exceptions to this were the parents from Overlea Comprehensive School, whose children were participating in the home–school reading initiative and were experiencing difficulty at school. Six out of seven pupils were helped with their homework, and in four instances this was a regular, time-consuming commitment. Those who gave prolonged help were not happy with the situation, but did so because as one couple described it, "he gets very distressed and uptight when he can't manage to do the work that has been set".

The teachers differed in their views about the purpose of homework and the role that parents should play. Within a year group in just one school, the teachers' views ranged from stating that parents should not do the work for their children, to seeing homework, at its best, as a joint exercise between home and school. The most common response (from about half the teachers) was that parents should 'service' the homework, for example, providing an appropriate environment for work to be undertaken, showing interest in what was undertaken and offering encouragement.

Views were sought on the desirability of formalizing parental involvement by means of joint homework assignments specifically designed for pupils and parents to work on together. The parents were not generally in favour of such assignments, although in one school a quarter, and in two, a third would like this form of contact. Of those who were in favour, the value of being involved in detailed work and of being able to help were stressed, but several expressed points of concern. Those who were not in favour emphasized that the time was not available and that it would be unfair on pupils whose parents did not take part for one reason or another.

The vast majority of teachers did not see potential in this development and had no plans to establish it. There were, however, a handful of staff who were extremely positive about the possible benefits. One teacher was working towards a cross-curricular project that would mean drawing on parents' own experiences; and one acting headteacher saw parents working with their own children as the logical conclusion of a serious commitment to involving parents in schools and something that the school should be working towards.

When asked about homework diaries, parents emphasized the need for them to be used efficiently by all involved, and frustration was expressed by those who did not receive clear information about what had been set. Some parents who regularly signed them were unclear about what they were signing because the diary was not explicit. As one father explained: "If I don't know exactly what has been set, I can't be sure that it has been completed." A common response was that the usefulness of the diaries was questionable, given the *laissez-faire* approach to their completion.

The staff were generally of the opinion that homework diaries were potentially useful, although they were frequently not used to the full effect by the adults concerned. One acting headteacher saw a homework diary as a way to "bring the parents into the learning process" and said that he was "constantly amazed by how many do use it". The system was described by a teacher as "as strong as the group tutor". They needed to be properly 'policed' if they were to have any value; and they were used to record work that was going home and not (with the exception of the record books used in the home–school reading project) for communication on wider issues.

The material presented above shows some of the differences in attitude and approach that emerged when parents and teachers were asked for their views on various aspects of contact between home and school in relation to individual children. In the next sections three schemes specifically designed to foster parents working with their own children are considered in detail.

Overlea Comprehensive School's Home–School Reading Project for first-year pupils experiencing difficulty

Parents' response to this involvement

The parents taking part in the shared reading initiative were well aware (with one exception) that their children were experiencing difficulty with reading. The invitation to partici-pate in the scheme was generally very well received and was seen as a logical move, designed to help the children overcome a specific problem. One mother who reported feeling "a mix-ture of slight unease and a feeling that I really ought to go to anything that might help him" typified the general attitude. None of the parents had considered not taking part themselves, and all but one of the children were said by their parents to be happy about their participating in this way.

The parents' awareness of their children's difficulties and appreciation at being invited to work with the school was in stark contrast to their reflections on their children's experiences in primary schools. Parents felt that in these schools they had not been kept informed of their children's reading development and had not been given an opportunity to help to remedy their lack of progress. The parents felt that the secondary school was seriously attempting to deal with their children's difficulties, although none of them knew how much extra help was being given to them.

The meetings

All seven children had been represented at the first meeting designed to introduce the shared reading (three by both parents), and all but one had attended themselves. The parents were positive about both the style and content of the meeting and had found it enjoyable and informative. One parent explained that "they were trying to make reading fun and up until then, for Ben, it hadn't been fun". Another gave details of techniques that had been explained and said that the meeting had helped her to develop patience. Some parents also welcomed the opportunity to show their children that they were concerned and willing to be involved.

Attendance at the meeting held at the end of the project was not so high, with only one child being represented by both parents and four others by one parent. Four children had attended. The parents said that it had been useful to hear other people's experiences and to draw support from those who were, as one set of parents said, "all in the same boat".

Staff wanted to convey to parents that they should be positive with children as they were struggling to read. One said that they were trying to offer parents "realistic possibilities" rather than "telling people that they should do things like us". They both felt that the meetings were enjoyable and emphasized their role in terms of keeping parents' morale up. One teacher said she thought that parents felt less isolated and drew support from each other as a result of the meetings.

Nevertheless, both teachers were dissatisfied with the style of the meetings. They did not want teacher-led groups and felt that it was difficult for people to sit and discuss things in the way that they had intended. One expressed unease about the role play they had done, simulating a parent and child reading together, and felt that it was ineffective (although amusing) and that it should be replaced by a video featuring a real situation.

Documentation

Parents were asked about the guidance sheets and record booklets that had been given out at the first meeting. Favourable comments were made about the information conveyed on the sheet. One mother had, for example, appreciated learning that she should praise her son as he was reading and not just when he finished.

The parents had all used the record booklets regularly except for the mother whose child had not wished to take part and, in this case, it had only been used once. Parents emphasized their appreciation of written feedback from staff. One mother felt that her own contributions had helped her because writing about progress had made her think constructively about her son's reading.

The teachers both saw value in the record booklets and welcomed the opportunity to write to parents on small issues. One said that she would always try to encourage with her comments, while the other saw value in making practical suggestions.

The pupils

Six of the seven pupils taking part were interviewed in school. They had enjoyed the evening meetings and were happy to be visited at home. They saw the shared reading as a project lasting for a few weeks that had resulted in their reading more than they normally would; they were enthusiastic about the books used during the project and could all elaborate on the story or content of their current one.

They explained that reading was not a priority for them and, while they knew they 'had to do it', it would only be undertaken at somebody else's suggestion. However, they were clearly concerned about their difficulty with reading and happy to take part in a scheme that might help.

The pupils' reading

Over the six-week period of the project, six of the seven children were said by their parents to have read with them at least five nights a week, which indicates a high level of commitment given the children's previous reluctance and lack of interest in reading. Reading was sometimes a fraught activity. One father explained that he had only read with his daughter twice because he does not "have the patience to do it more often". The time spent on shared reading each day by the families varied from five to 20 minutes.

There was a pattern to the reading sessions, in that most of the parents would read some of the story as an introduction and then the child would read to them. There was a general concern that because of their struggles with reading, the children were unable to follow a story and so parents tried to read enough to make it 'flow'. Most of the children were said to settle well to the sessions. One mother explained that the sessions had simply "become routine", and a father felt that his son "put himself out a bit because of the project".

Three children had read one or two books during the six weeks and three had read more. The parents were generally pleased with the books selected and were aware of the need to capture the children's interest. One mother explained that the teachers "made every effort to do this with Stephen. He's football mad and that might account for part of the interest he had for the whole project." Several football books had been available from school for the project. The two teachers said that finding books of an appropriate level for 11-year-olds who found reading difficult was a problem. They both emphasized the importance of the children themselves choosing which book to take home. They bought books about children's specific interests from bookshops and hoped to motivate them to want to read. If children chose books that were difficult for them, they were not dissuaded, but a comment to that effect was made in the record book.

Outcomes of the project

The parents were generally convinced of the benefits of the reading project. Only one family, excluding the girl who did not wish to participate in the reading at home, did not feel that involvement had had any direct benefits for their child. The other parents saw clear gains in terms of changes in attitude and in self-confidence. One couple said that their daughter had had a "general lift" and had benefited from feeling involved in something special which had meant extra individual attention. The strongest supporting statement came from the parents who said that they did not know how their daughter "would have coped without something like this". They, in turn, felt more confident themselves about trying to help their children and were reassured about the difficulty they were experiencing.

Both teachers agreed that the project had resulted in a change of attitude in the pupils involved. They felt that they were now more positive about books and more motivated to try. One teacher recalled hearing a child recommending a book to another and said that to have that exchange between two poor readers was "what it's all about". The teachers did not wish to evaluate the project solely by using reading test scores because they were convinced, by the changes in motivation and attitude, of the value of the project. Nevertheless, some of the children taking part were tested, and all four of those for whom a pre- and post-project comparison could be made had improved their score, although of course these increases may have been unrelated to involvement in the shared reading initiative.

The head of department described this project as "almost departmental policy now" and would like to run a similar scheme annually. Both teachers believed that a short period of intervention was best in order to motivate parents without imposing too much of a burden, and to enable realistic goals to be set. They were keen to avoid parents feeling guilty, and acknowledged how hard it could be "to find that ten minutes each day". One said that she would not describe some of the families involved as "bookish" and hoped that the project had the effect of "leaving a door open with lights on the other side". The other teacher wondered about a more structured continuation and thought that they could start the project again in the third year to "re-charge people who might need it".

Millshire LEA's Home–School Reading Initiative in primary schools

Attendance at workshops

The workshops held in the five schools included in this study (where parents and children worked together in class) were well attended by children. The take-up rates ranged from "initially every child" to "between 30 and 40 per cent". Of the 53 parents providing information about the workshops, one-quarter said they had attended all or nearly all of those on offer and a few said alternate weeks or were unsure of the number. Most had been to between five and ten sessions a term. The figures showed a fairly regular pattern of attendance.

Children and workshops

The vast majority of parents said that their children enjoyed the workshops and that they had benefited from attending. One-quarter of parents said this was because the workshops provided an opportunity for parent and child to work together without interruption or the demands of family life. Another quarter focused on the fact that children took delight in home and school coming together in this way. One parent referred to her child 'enjoying seeing me in school. It has bridged the gap between home and school life.'

Interestingly, less than one-quarter of parents saw the benefits principally in terms of formal 'learning'. One comment saw the workshops as "helping with his reading and understanding of letters and sounds". The other parents detected a change in attitude. One child was now said to "tolerate losing a game to others", while other comments referred to gains in confidence and concentration span.

In relation to the activities undertaken in workshops, nearly all of the parents said that they already played card and board games at home with their children. Most had not changed the frequency of playing since attending the workshops, while eight now played games more frequently. There was a similar figure for reading, in that six parents said that they read with their children more frequently as a result of attending the workshops.

The teachers said that children enjoyed having parents come to school in this way and that such contact would have an impact on their school work. The disadvantages were seen mainly in terms of children whose parents did not turn up or who "give up", so that children are left "feeling disappointed".

Children whose parents do not attend

Over half of the parents agreed that it was distressing for children whose parents did not come to the workshops and two-fifths said they were unsure. Only four did not feel it was a problem. Meantime staff in all schools were conscious of children 'missing out'. In some schools, children were able to work with surrogates, in others they stayed in class with their teacher or joined other groups. In some situations, a mixed approach was used with some surrogates and some children staying together as a group.

Parents attending workshops

The vast majority of parents said they had enjoyed the workshops, the most popular choice of activity being "project work on a topic, for example dinosaurs/flowers". Some parents would have liked the opportunity for a quiet time to read with their children in workshops, and a few would have liked to play board games or do art and craft work.

Nearly three-fifths of the parents felt that they had learnt from attending the workshops, and several of them considered they had gained an insight into how work was undertaken in school. These responses showed respect for the work undertaken by class teachers and for the methods used.

A number of parents reported their new awareness of how children learn or of ways to teach them. Going to workshops had also allowed parents to see their children in quite a different light. One mother said she had learnt "what my son enjoys, what he is good at and what he finds difficult", and another that "my son is more capable than he lets on".

Parents felt that going to the workshops made it easier for them to approach teachers to discuss their concerns or ask questions, and also made them feel more relaxed in school. Nearly two-fifths agreed that it was unreasonable to expect parents to attend regular workshops in school, one-fifth were unsure and the remainder felt that such a regular commitment was acceptable. Just over three-fifths of parents said that provision should be made in school for babies and toddlers to be cared for during the workshops, while nearly one-fifth disagreed and the same number were unsure.

Parents were invited to add any further comments they wished to make about this sort of contact with schools, and three-fifths chose to do so. Most spoke very positively of the workshops, although some practical suggestions for improvements or reservations that the parents had about workshops were expressed. One mother's comment summed up the concerns of some parents:

> I felt under a great deal of pressure to produce a board game, although my child was not interested. We got part-way through the second project and decided between us that my son would benefit far more from being taught in the smaller class, while the rest were doing the

workshop. His comment was that he would rather be doing maths in the classroom.

The main advantage for parents, as the teachers saw it, was the opportunity to see how work was tackled in school. It was anticipated that parents would be more positive about school as a result. There were also comments about parents having access to school resources, about their "learning how hard learning is" and about enabling them to meet other parents.

The teachers thought the biggest problem for parents was their having to make a regular commitment of time. As one teacher explained, "I think some might feel under a lot of pressure to come and they may think if they don't come their child's language progression won't be there". A rather different point was made by the teacher who was conscious of mothers who "just haven't been able to cope with what was expected and have felt embarrassed by failing in front of other people".

Outcomes of workshops for teachers

Teachers emphasized the beneficial effect this contact had on relationships between parents and teachers. One typical response was:

> I think it has broken down barriers. I think they see us differently. They see that we aren't any different. I think they also realized how much work we put into the workshops and we are definitely working together. Parents do want to help.

Teachers also felt able to plan detailed individual work that could not otherwise have been undertaken because it was so labour-intensive.

The main disadvantage for teachers was that preparing for and organizing this work was very time-consuming. The support available from the advisory teacher is discussed in Chapter 8. The workshops themselves also obviously generated work. One teacher estimated that it took a half-hour each session to "put on the urn, bring in the milk, sort out the coffee money, etc.". She estimated spending "a good few hours each week" on activities such as planning, making and mending games, and checking records.

The main point that emerged when teachers were asked about any advice they would give to colleagues was the need to allow plenty of time for planning and to have adequate support, both from within school and outside. One teacher urged colleagues to "plan carefully and have an open mind", to "seek support", to use "other people and other people's expertise" and to "think very hard about the best way to communicate [to parents] exactly what is involved". Another teacher said, "keep it small and really think out what you are going to do". On a practical point, one teacher stressed that "you need a lot of resources and a head who is willing to allow you to use paper, books, etc.".

Five staff identified ways in which the workshops had influenced them. Teachers in one school spoke of having learnt what parents can give to their own children with time and of having been helped to see what individual children need. Another teacher's comments on what she herself had learnt from this type of involvement with parents is worth quoting in full because of wider implications:

> I've learnt more about what parents think about school and what they expect from school. A lot of parents don't have any idea about what goes on in school and I think that a lot of parents don't even begin to imagine how children learn. Many parents think we teach in the way they were taught. That we write everything on the blackboard and the children copy it down. We don't explain what we are doing – we are bad as a profession for doing this, and we are particularly bad here. We should explain every aspect of the school to parents. I also think to have these open channels of communication with parents gets criticism out in to the open. I don't like the chit-chat at the gate.

Parental involvement in the process of choosing GCSE options in Marksbury Comprehensive School

The decision

Half of the parents interviewed said that their sons or daughters had had strong feelings about the options which they would choose as they embarked on their third year in the school. Only one parent, however, claimed to have had a definite preference for specific options to be taken by her son. A more typical response was that of a mother who said they had "talked a lot about the idea that he had to choose and why he had to choose. It's a lot for a child of that age and we didn't want to push."

Nevertheless, all the parents wanted some involvement in the decision, even if it was at the level of being kept informed of what their children were being asked to decide. They had all talked to their children about the options. In some instances, this had obviously been no more than taking an interest in what they were doing; and in others, it was a discussion of which subjects would be useful for a subsequent career. But in all cases, it was said that the final decision on what was stated on the option form had been made by their children. The fact that the 'real' final decision rested with the school caused alarm among some parents, who did not know at the time of the interviews what options their children would be taking. One father already knew that his daughter had had to re-think her choices, and so far as he was concerned, "if the options offered initially do not come to anything, it seems to defeat the object of having a choice".

Contact with the school

Some parents' comments on the school's booklets about options and on the meeting held at this time are recorded in Chapter 4. There were two other occasions when the parents were invited into school. One of these was a consultation session which was held about a month after the meeting, but not one parent who had attended said that their child's options had been discussed. In contrast, all the parents who attended the evening session some four months later, when the completed option form was discussed with the form tutor, were generally very positive about this meeting. Apart from complaints about how long some of them had had to wait, they all agreed that their attendance had been useful. In some cases, this was because it gave them the reassurance that the options chosen were reasonable; but in others, parents wanted tutors to reinforce the advice that they themselves had given. Overall, the parents thought that they had had sufficient opportunities to make contact with members of staff during this time.

Parental understanding of GCSE and modular courses

While many parents felt that they had an adequate understanding of the GCSE system, a minority still had problems in understanding what exactly would be expected of their children. For some parents, the main concern was about how much pressure their children would be under because of the emphasis on coursework. Not all parents felt that they could have gone to the teachers for guidance. This father was not alone in his views:

> I don't think some teachers are clear. They may know how their own subject works but they have not got a clue about other subjects. If teachers don't know, how can parents, no matter how many booklets they send home? If you ask a specific question, they will tell you to see the teacher concerned – and that is fine if you can see the teacher on the night or you can come up to the school again, but I don't think there can be many people who feel very confident with GCSE at the moment.

The tutors were asked for their views on parental involvement in general during this time and on other aspects of the process. All were in favour of parents being involved in their children's decisions and of schools providing sufficient information to enable them to do so. While some teachers thought that parents needed more detailed explanations about options, including talks on the nature of GCSE and of modules, the majority felt that sufficient information was given to parents, and the curriculum coordinator, in particular, opposed any change. Tutors favoured the idea of encouraging parents to engage in a discussion of possible options during the consultation sessions. All said they had tried to do this but had not always been successful.

Discussion

It was clear that, in most cases, parents were not routinely brought into their children's learning by schools. Staff were generally willing to respond to parents' overtures and to deal with them informally on an individual basis. To go further was seen by many as 'putting pressure on' and 'inequitable', in that it would give advantages to those who least needed them. On the other hand, the responses of parents suggested that many opportunities were being lost to bring home and school together in children's learning; the *ad hoc* approach left many parents confused and in fact favoured those who were most at ease in school.

The findings did not substantiate the teachers' view that the parents who were interested 'came and asked', and that not coming into school indicated a lack of interest. The statements made by some teachers concerning parents' motivation and aims were not supported by the information collected from parents about their aspirations for their children and their desire for them to achieve in school.

While the idea of parents coming into school to work with their own children was not received enthusiastically by many parents or teachers, the positive responses of those currently engaged in this practice sounded an optimistic note for those who might wish to develop this work. They were not experiencing the problems identified by those speaking hypothetically about the idea. Given the widespread reluctance and the reservations expressed, a good deal of groundwork will be required in relation both to parents and teachers before this practice can become widespread.

Staff who agree with the principle of involving parents in their children's reading, but who are uneasy about putting pressure on parents to take books home, may be able to capitalize further on the interest in sharing books with their children that parents professed. Teachers underestimated both the parents' desire to help their children in this way and the extent to which it was already being done. Parents were unsure about what to do in relation to reading development, even if they had been reading to their children from an early age; general statements about 'reading anything' confused them. Involving parents in their children's reading was undertaken in an *ad hoc* way and there was variation within schools in terms of which books went home and when. Encouraging parental support with reading may have great potential – particularly in view of the point several teachers made about the difficulty they had in finding enough time within the busy school day to hear children read as frequently as they would like.

The information about activities to continue at home and guidance for parents about what they could do with their children illustrated teachers' reluctance to initiate these forms of contact, yet a significant proportion of parents said that they would find them useful. Future developments will be blocked unless attitudes change. It is of interest that unanimous support for the idea of activities to do at home came from parents attending workshops in Millshire, who would have had an above average access to activities. Of the 'least positive' parent group (whose children had just started at Tatehill First School), it is worth noting their generally positive views on the pre-school activity packs they had received from the school and speculating that they might value material for older pupils as their children settled.

The findings highlighted potential areas of confusion about homework, even when there was a consensus that work should be done outside school. Without a clear policy on such work, the scene was set for misunderstandings and, in some cases, frustration. Staff must be clear about the purpose of homework, plan such work carefully and must communicate their intent to parents. A few individuals were extremely positive about extending the role of parents through joint homework assignments, and they saw great potential in this. Any such developments would need to be undertaken with realistic expectations of the time and effort required.

More efficient channels of communication between home and school in relation to homework seemed to have general approval. Potentially, the diaries could serve as vehicles for creating a dialogue to discuss issues pertaining to individual children, as well as listing work that had been set for a particular night.

The home-reading initiative in Overlea Comprehensive School left most of the involved adults convinced that the structure it imposed had changed parents' behaviour in relation to reading and had positive outcomes in relation to the children's reading ability. The key elements of this project were that parents were invited to participate in a systematic, but not unrealistically onerous, way in their children's learning. They received support, reassurance and some practical help. The children experienced a short-term 'boost', which the adults saw as having longer-term implications with regard to self-confidence and motivation.

This initiative was well received and offers a useful model for helping children with reading difficulties: the parents were pleased with the way the project had been organized, and the informality and efforts of staff to make them feel welcome were appreciated; and the work was clearly thought-out and methods and goals communicated to parents. Parents felt supported in their concern about the difficulties their children were experiencing, sometimes in striking contrast to how they had been dealt with in the primary schools their children had attended.

The workshops in primary schools in Millshire were valuable in themselves and were said to have improved contact between home and school. By carefully structuring the session and formalizing the way in which parents were said to gain 'insights', there may be more of this 'learning about school' that the teachers espoused and, certainly, some parents said had been achieved. Teachers spent a great deal of time organizing the sessions and could, perhaps, run fewer sessions with more precise aims and objectives. The need to identify goals, develop strategies to achieve them and respond to parents' views and experiences was striking. Now to do so resulted in frustration and wasted efforts on both sides.

The fact that some parents had learnt a considerable amount about their children's capabilities and how they were learning in school in the course of the workshops was interesting on two counts. It was clear that parents appreciated receiving this kind of information, and that they were not getting enough of it from other more routine channels of communication.

The practical arrangements for the workshops could usefully be reviewed in the light of experience. Regular weekly workshops were difficult for some parents. It is possible that fortnightly/monthly sessions for each child, designed to suit individual parents, would be just as effective. The children enjoyed having their parents in school, and parents were willing to take on the commitment, but many would appreciate greater flexibility and child care for younger siblings would be welcomed.

The parents from Marksbury Comprehensive School expressed their desire to be involved in their children's option choices and valued the opportunities they had had to discuss the decision and to hear the teachers' views and advice. Their comments highlight the very complex nature of some of the issues parents have to tackle if they are to make a realistic contribution to their children's experiences in school.

Taken together, the work presented in this chapter shows that it would be worthwhile to develop a variety of ways of involving parents in the curriculum with their children. Many parents would welcome this because much current practice discourages and confuses them. Opportunities to draw the learning environments of home and school together are being lost. However, it is clear that many schools will have to re-think and evaluate the purpose of their work with parents, and it is equally clear that considerable groundwork will be required if initiatives in this field are to 'take root'.

4 Meetings for Parents

Introduction

Staff in the schools included in this research held parents' meetings which varied in form, content and purpose. There were lectures, courses, workshops, discussion groups and committee meetings. Some meetings were designed to convey information about how schools were approaching the curriculum, others were designed to launch parental involvement schemes and still others gave parents the opportunity to express their views on, and discuss, broader educational issues. The first Annual Parents' Meetings, for example, were held by governors during 1987, following legislation the previous year.

A major point to emerge from the study of meetings for parents was how difficult it was to present and convey information about school policy and practice in a productive and accessible form. Staff need well-developed communication skills if they are to undertake this task, either on paper or through meetings, and if they are to enter into the more ambitious dialogue with parents that was attempted in some schools. The activities discussed here highlighted the potential gains of a variety of meetings and illustrated some of the pitfalls and limitations of some of the approaches to this form of contact. They show how easily the intentions of staff can be misunderstood by parents and vice versa.

Meetings on the curriculum

There were instances where information about practice was presented clearly and valued by the recipients; such details had given them an insight into their children's work and experience. Evening meetings about the policy on reading in an infant school in Planeborough contained some of these elements; by explaining the extent to which reading-related activities (as opposed to actually hearing children read) featured in the infants' timetable, teachers had clarified the position for parents. Explanation of the different colour codes appearing on the school's books meant that parents could use them in the way that staff had intended.

Just over two-thirds of the mothers (and no fathers) of children in the nursery at another infant school in Planeborough had attended a course of six, weekly sessions. Two of the meetings had a workshop format, where the parents undertook mathematics, language and creative activities. The other sessions were spent in classrooms, where parents could see how the reception children's work was organized, and they were encouraged to help the children with their activities.

The mothers welcomed the opportunity to be involved in this way and saw the sessions as enabling them to help their children at home and aiding their understanding of the system in school: they had gained a new understanding of how the children were taught. The school had recently established an open-plan layout where children changed classrooms for different activities; initially, parents had been sceptical of this arrangement, but changed their views when they had the opportunity to spend time in the rearranged classrooms. For example, one mother said that originally she had thought, "what a ridiculous situation, why can't they just leave it as it was, but I mean now I see that everybody has benefited from them doing it that way, even the teachers".

The course had whetted the parents' appetite for more information. One of them said, for example, that although the head-teacher had claimed not to have any "non-readers" in the school, "parents would like to understand more of what goes on, so that they can help". Two themes emerged from these parents' responses: the realization that they had learnt a great deal about how their children are taught; and that they would have liked to have had such knowledge earlier on, especially those whose nursery-age child was their youngest.

However, these meetings in both schools also served to point up some complexities. At the evening meetings on reading, information was conveyed via lectures from staff, with the opportunity for some questions at the end, and the limitations of this approach were clear. School policy was presented as an unalterable fact without explanation or discussion, which sometimes left parents confused and with unanswered queries. Firm policy statements about not using phonics in the infant school were an example of this, and indicated the need to acknowledge and value what parents may have been doing with their children already. Similarly, the parents of nursery children who attended the six-week course were left feeling guilty about the activities they had, or had not, done with their children, and this was both unfair and counter-productive. As one mother explained: "I've learned that I've been teaching Hugh wrong for four years, teaching him the wrong way to do his reading and all sorts. I've just been told it's completely wrong. He's got to do it all over again."

The teachers believed that home–school communication was improved by the course but seemed unaware of the mixed reactions parents had experienced. It is crucial that staff are aware of the impact their statements can have: one headteacher's assertion that the first five years of life were the vital ones for intellectual growth and development, and that the years that followed could only attempt to rectify what children had 'missed' in the pre-school phase, was not only misleading, but disheartening when presented to parents whose children were already past that stage.

Meetings on school policy and practice

The headteachers' questionnaire provided information about Annual Parents' Meetings, and parents and staff in the case studies were asked for their views on and experience of these events. The meetings were not well attended (less than one-fifth of pupils were represented by their parents).

Just under half of the headteachers felt that the meetings would be of value. The most common response was that it would be useful to have the opportunity to discuss issues and increase this type of communication between home and school. And one typical comment was that the meetings had created 'an open forum for school–parent discussion and information which must, by its nature, be of value'.

Other headteachers focused on the Annual Parents' Meetings as an opportunity to inform parents and increase their understanding of how the school functions. One wrote that this was 'because parents need to know, understand and support the work that is done in school', and another that the meetings 'would help parents to understand the aims and objectives of the school and its short-term priorities'.

Only a few headteachers saw a more pro-active role for parents, in that the meetings were an opportunity for teachers and governors to learn from them and hear their views. One headteacher said that he was 'encouraged by the range of ideas presented by the parents for the future', and another that such a meeting would be valuable 'if we use it to discuss and identify parents' hopes for their children's education'.

A rather different slant came from those who emphasized the effect that such meetings could have on the role and function of governors. This point was made by the headteacher who wrote, 'It will concentrate governors' minds on their role and, hopefully, make them effective and conscientious, thereby benefiting the school', and by the one who saw the meetings as 'a means of communication and evidence that governors are "real" people with powers to influence the life of the school and essentially are interested in the education system'.

Of the headteachers who did not see value in the meetings, the most common response was that many parents would not attend and poor levels of attendance were cited to support this. Slightly fewer responses focused on the headteachers' belief that as parents had open access to the school anyway, such meetings were superfluous. Those in this group confidently asserted that parents' needs for contact and information were fully met. One headteacher wrote that 'the parents are in every day to bring/take their children home as well as to help and so they know all that is going on and ask questions, complain, express worries as the situation crops up'.

When teachers in some schools selected for case-study work were asked for their views on Annual Parents' Meetings, rather more than one-half said that they saw value in them. However, most of those who answered positively indicated that the value of these meetings lay in their potential rather than in what they were currently seen to achieve. Those who expressed unqualified support for Annual Parents' Meetings saw their benefits as twofold, namely that they could be seen as one other strand of parental contact, and another opportunity to give parents more information. It was hoped that such meetings could be made more welcoming and less formal, and that the reports distributed prior to the meeting could be less full of "teacherese" and jargon.

Those teachers who saw no value in Annual Parents' Meetings focused on the low numbers of parents attending. The meetings were seen as "a mere formality" and the low levels of attendance were said to indicate that this type of meeting was not of interest to most parents, especially as parental attendance could be very much higher at other types of home–school meetings.

In some schools, there were other meetings which gave parents the opportunity to discuss policy and practice. In the community primary school in Planeborough, elected parent representatives comprised three-quarters of the Community Association Committee which ran the community programme under the leadership of a community director and the head-teacher. In an infant school in Planeborough, working parties of parents had been involved in deciding school policy on multiculturalism, swimming, safety and in the production of a school handbook. The parents who were involved in these decisions had been selected by teachers and parent governors.

In another school, a headteacher organized a meeting for primary school parents on the Education Reform Act 1988 (then the Education Reform Bill). This meeting was repeated on three occasions and LEA advisers and more than 100 parents took part. Activities to stimulate consideration of the school curriculum and parental involvement were undertaken in small groups. Teacher appraisal, open enrolment, the National Curriculum, methods of assessment, opting-out and the increasing responsibility of governors were discussed in the course of the evening, and the advisers and the headteacher answered questions as they arose. The headteacher anticipated that the evenings would raise awareness of the considerable changes taking place in education and how they would affect what schools were providing.

All parents and staff were welcome at the Parents' Consultative Group in Pendinge Comprehensive, which met approximately once a month; attendance varied but had been as high as 70 people. The humanities, tutors and tutoring, the Technical and Vocational Education Initiative (TVEI), AIDS, the English curriculum and the school's resources were among the topics discussed, and concerns which the parents had expressed were aired and incorporated into future plans.

Communicating with parents

The effective provision of information to parents requires a well-considered approach. The production of clearly written, accessible information that spells out the main points to be discussed at subsequent meetings, but in such a form that it is also free-standing, is vital. The right tone is extremely difficult to attain: the parents' response to the two GCSE booklets in Marksbury Comprehensive School clearly illustrated this. Several of them described how complex they were; a few parents had been asked to comment on the drafts of both booklets and had found them very confusing:

> I think we are quite articulate and very interested in our children's education. It isn't just this school. I think it might be that when schools try to explain things, they can't believe parents know so little and need so much guidance... They [the staff] said parents like the visual effects, they like all the pictures and diagrams but I thought some of that was confusing.

The booklets had been modified in the light of parents' comments but reservations remained. Many parents still thought they were too complicated – and that too much information was given too quickly.

The style could possibly have been improved by consulting parents other than those who were chosen because they were seen to be 'articulate'. It would also be of value to present the documents to staff as a topic for discussion, rather than as a completed project in which they had been insufficiently involved, and to prepare materials for parents in community languages.

The meeting held when third-year pupils were making their decisions about the GCSEs they wished to study was well attended. However, staff and parents both expressed their concern that in order for the evening to stand any chance of success, the parents needed to have read and understood the booklets produced by the school on GCSE options. It was generally accepted that this material was highly complex.

Oral presentations are equally difficult to pitch successfully. Conveying facts, for example, the colour coding of reading books, has obvious merit but other matters, ranging from school policy on phonics to the implications of the Education Reform Act 1988, require more than a one-way passage of information. Meetings need to encourage discussion and give some explanation for the reasoning and evidence that have led to decisions. As one parent of an infant school child, who thought that a fuller analysis of the methods used should have been given at the meeting she attended, explained, "They did not bother about spelling and said they were only worried to get ideas down on paper. That is fine, but there was no attempt to deal with parents' concerns about the more formal aspects like spelling and presentation."

Some parents from Marksbury Comprehensive School said that they would have liked to have been told more facts about GCSE in the meeting which they had attended. Even though this mother felt she already had a good grasp of the new exam, she thought more information should have been provided:

> We'd had to comment on the booklets and talk to Mr Madeley about GCSEs. We'd also read all the *Sunday Times* supplements on the exam. With that background, I think what they gave us was very poor. I don't think the communication was very good. It must have been very difficult for the teachers because it was the first time, but it was not very informative and I don't think all parents knew why they were there. I think they thought they were going to be told something, and I think the school wanted the parents to drag it out of the teachers, but the parents just didn't know where to begin.

And there was also, among some parents who had attended, concern about certain teachers' inability to deal with those areas which were worrying them. They appreciated that it was reasonably new to teachers, but they were worried about any risks that may be taken with their children's futures. A particular concern related to the extent to which GCSE courses prepared students for A-level courses. In one case, the tutor had said that the modular science course would be an adequate preparation for any of the sciences taken in the sixth form. It was known that the head of chemistry did not agree with this and some parents had left the meeting feeling perplexed. Other parents, like this mother, thought that fundamental points had not been answered: "Some of us were worried about what would happen if a child was off for a longish period and missed work or a large part of a module. They couldn't answer that, they skated around it and said they would try to come to an arrangement."

Some meetings were, however, designed with the intention of stimulating discussion. The meetings about the Education Reform Act 1988 provided the opportunity for informal debate, and parents' comments and questions were taken seriously and responded to. Written information was circulated to parents prior to the meeting. Clearly, such activities make significant demands on staff and require considerable preparation and planning. Sometimes such demands may be excessive: staff in Marksbury Comprehensive School were expected to discuss with parents the implications of the GCSE and its assessment procedures at an early stage in its implementation, originally with little support from senior colleagues. Some of them found this an extremely daunting task, and one which undermined both the quality of home–school relations and the teachers' desire to make contact with parents in this way.

In the event, a senior teacher accompanied each tutor and so was on hand to answer questions if necessary. Most of the tutors thought the meetings had been worthwhile, even though one of them described it as the "most frightening experience that I've ever had". The meetings helped another tutor to re-assess her views on parents, particularly on those whom she had judged to be not so interested in their children's school work:

> I was very pleased to see such a good response from my particular group. Some of the parents I was surprised to see. I did feel, however, that I became defensive. I was surprised at the interest they had taken – and I know that sounds like a very patronizing thing to say. I had not realized how worried they might be about their children's futures and their chances when they left school.

Only one teacher from Woodvale's Home–School Liaison Committee emphasized its potential for achieving a dialogue, describing the meetings as a "two-way filter system". In general, teachers did not discuss external constraints on their work frankly, and tended to defend their position rather than share their concerns, for example, in the discussion about assessment for GCSE. Similarly, there was little evidence of staff systematically seeking parents' views and responses. Indeed, their perceptions of these were often at odds with the reality.

It is important to view meetings as part of a continuing channel of communication and exchange of views. Rather than viewing meetings as the solution, it would be helpful to see them as opening up opportunities for questions and discussions; because parents obviously have views and insights that could be conveyed where such channels existed.

Aims of meetings

As well as getting the approach right, it is vitally important to be clear about the desired outcome of the contact. This lack of clarity was most starkly illustrated by some curriculum evenings where little seemed to have been achieved. The evenings were unstructured, with work and books on display, and teachers available for discussion. The few parents who attended would have gained very little and may indeed have felt reluctant, because of this experience, to attend future events. The letter inviting them to attend had stated that the sessions would 'help you to help your children with their work at home'. The purpose of the sessions had not been clearly presented to parents, or adequately prepared for by staff. This was a striking example of the well-meaning, potentially productive, work that went no way near meeting the very ambitious goal of informing parents about the curriculum, so that they would be able to help their children. On the whole, parents spent a brief period wandering around the classroom flicking through the resources on display and exchanging a few words (which were not supposed to be about their own children's progress) with staff.

The Parents' Consultative Group at Pendinge Comprehensive School provided an opportunity for staff to hear parents' views and experiences on a variety of topics. Misunderstandings about homework were aired and the efforts and hard work of staff were commended. But again, careful thought needs to be given to the purpose and outcomes of such gatherings. The need for clear ground rules was evident. If individual members of staff are identified publicly in their absence – in a sense, 'reported' – this will affect not only the tone of the meeting, but the attitude of staff towards parents having access to school in this way.

The School Policy Advisory Group in Lane End Infants School was well received by the few parents who had attended meetings. Parents' attitudes to such events are rather complex – as one 'non-attender' explained, such meetings were not for her because "you would have to be outspoken and I'm not that way inclined". But another mother felt that such discussions gave "an insight into what the head and the teachers think, so that you get to know them a little bit more as people", and that they were valuable "in principle, in that things should be public".

Most of the teachers saw the School Policy Advisory Group as valuable and important in giving parents a voice "to say what they feel about central issues". It enabled parents to gain an "insight into how the school works", so that they could feel that they were partners in the education of their children. The most positive response came from the teacher who was uneasy that "so much goes on behind closed doors" and said that it would be valuable for parents to realize that many decisions were imposed on schools by the local authority.

Attendance at meetings

Some parents made considerable efforts to attend sessions in school, coming straight from work or rearranging domestic matters, and may well be discouraged from making such plans again if meetings are uninformative and badly organized. Poor levels of attendance were common and, while recognizing the considerable efforts already made by some staff and also the enormous barriers which still have to be overcome, there were some pointers for change in the meetings studied. Schools may foster the formation of cliques, which can exclude new members or wider participation at an early stage. There were examples of parents being selected for working parties or for consultation in a way that exacerbated this; parents who attended meetings were sometimes treated in a way that may serve to widen the divide. They were referred to at meetings as those who were 'interested', or indeed those who 'cared'.

A majority of those interviewed from Woodvale School thought that the Home–School Liaison Committee succeeded in informing interested parents about the school, but the poor attendance at organized events disappointed them. Some pointed to instances of personal success where children had been obviously pleased to see their parents involved, or where it had been made easier for them to approach a member of staff when a problem arose. But one mother who had in fact felt on the 'outside' of the committee during her membership thought that, while it was successful for those parents who were involved, it had little relevance for the majority:

> They [committee members] are a clique, and although I am sure they mean well, if they are not going to welcome an outsider into the committee...they are not going to welcome other parents... I realize that I could have done more, but I did feel outside that committee and I think the rest of the parent body would too.

Making sure that meetings are welcoming and acknowledging that coming in to school can be a daunting prospect for some parents would also help. The experience of a father who was 'lost' at the meeting in Marksbury Comprehensive School clearly illustrates how important good organization is; he explained:

> My wife had a previous appointment and couldn't go, and I was working late, so I arrived well after it had started. Darren had been on at me about going to the school, he said I had to go and all that. When I got there, they'd left the hall and I wandered around on my own. I couldn't find which room his tutor was in or anything. I know I was late, but I do think that was bad. I forgot to get the information off Darren before I left [home], but there was no one there to help me. I had a cup of tea and a biscuit and went home. I thought it was a big waste of time and I'd gone up specially when I was very busy, so I wasn't very pleased.

Overcoming these practical barriers requires time and planning. With limited resources and many other demands on teachers' time, it is easy to have a situation such as that in Woodvale Comprehensive School, where parents 'automatically' stayed on the Home–School Liaison Committee year after year. The levels of concern expressed about the small number of parents involved and the need to guard against the formation of a clique highlighted the need for a periodic critical review and evaluation of work with parents, so that practices that may at best be seen as a waste of time, and at worst may demoralize staff and confuse or alienate parents, are not allowed to continue.

The perceived value of meetings

The responses to the questions about Annual Parents' Meetings clearly illustrated the range of opinion that exists on the value of parents having this contact with school. Some headteachers were enthusiastic about this enhancement of their existing contact, while others regarded it as superfluous. It is interesting that many of those who did not see value in such meetings claimed that the opportunity to deal with 'problems' or 'concerns' was already there. By doing so, they focused squarely on these negatives and ignored the potential value of parents having group, rather than individual, contact with schools. Many of the respondents did not acknowledge that there could be general issues of interest that could most usefully be aired in a group situation. As one headteacher explained: 'Parents showing concern about the school come and find the answers on site.'

Setting such statements against the other findings of this research would necessitate treating with caution the suggestion that parents already have, and use, open access. The evidence was that many parents had unanswered questions and gaps in their knowledge. But it is also important to view the responses within the context of the possible development of this form of contact between home and school. Very few headteachers felt that Annual Parents' Meetings could provide an opportunity to learn from parents and hear their views.

The meetings attended and discussed during the course of this research indicate clearly the potential gains of extending this form of contact, and there are many issues which have to be addressed if the contact is to have the desired effect. The sessions must be well planned in terms of their aims and procedures and must be efficiently presented and executed.

To convey information coherently, concisely and at the right level, whether it be written or oral, is a challenge which has met with varying degrees of success. The more ambitious goal of establishing a dialogue would necessitate the allocation of time and resources and a significant commitment from staff.

5 Parental Involvement at Times of Transition

Introduction

At every stage in the educational system, children and young people experience change. When they start school, there is the separation from the parent or primary caregiver. Then there are moves from one class to the next and from sector to sector. Change is a normal part of life and of learning but there are potential difficulties as children leave behind that which is familiar. There is a consensus in the literature that the way change is managed is crucial, in both the immediate and longer term (see Jowett, 1989), and much attention has been given to ways of building bridges between the home and school to ease transitions.

During this research, a range of strategies employed by schools to help children adjust to change have been studied. These have included visits to the homes of pre-school and nursery children and to those of some first-year pupils in a comprehensive school; meetings in schools both before and after entry, where teachers explained their aims and practices to parents; videos designed to give parents a better idea of their children's school experiences; activity packs for parents to use with their pre-school children in the term before they start school; and demonstration lessons and curriculum evenings to give parents the opportunity to understand more about what goes on in the classroom. By providing these activities, schools are acknowledging not only that parents have the right to information about their children's education, but also that they will be better able to support their children through the period of change if they are familiar with the schools they are moving to.

Parents' and teachers' views on transition form the first part of this chapter. The process of transition was the focus in three of the schools selected for detailed case-study work. Tatehill First School and Banthorpe and Overlea Comprehensives all had induction programmes for new entrants and details of these are provided later in the chapter.

Parents' and teachers' views

Most parents were happy with the way their children had settled into school, but this is not to say that it was a trouble-free time. Problems of bullying, anxiety at starting somewhere new, establishing friendships and reacting to the demands made by a new school were mentioned by parents of primary and secondary school pupils. Many of these problems had been resolved quickly, and parents felt that most teachers were aware of the tensions arising from change.

It was not unusual for parents to say that they did not understand what went on in schools and how different it all seemed from their own school days. It was evident that many of them wanted to know more about their children's schools and about the curriculum, both at the primary and the secondary levels. Although many schools attempted to provide information at the time of the change as well as later, there was a tendency to describe the mechanics of their practice without explaining the rationale. There were parents who were not clear why some practices were undertaken, particularly when they were new to a school.

An instance of this emerged in the interviews with parents of children who had recently started at Overlea Comprehensive School. As part of the transition programme, the head of the first year invited all new pupils to her home in the course of the year. By the time of the interviews, 13 children had made such a visit and six others were arranged. Although parents thought it was a good idea and regarded it as a feature of what they considered to be the caring ethos of the school, a few expressed uncertainty about the rationale and benefit of such visits. While the value of these contacts was self-evident to the teacher concerned (as they gave her the opportunity to spend some time with a few children in a relaxed atmosphere and allowed them to get to know her better), it was not clear to all the parents as it had not been made explicit to them.

Some parents from Tatehill First School did not understand the reasons for particular policies. The school was a denominational one, drawing children from a wide catchment area. A school bus was available, but the parents were told that if their children were to use it, they would have to do so without being accompanied by parents from the second day of term. A number of parents living at some distance from the school found this rigidity unacceptable and decided to make their own arrangements for getting their five-year-olds to school. There was another 'rule' designed to foster children's independence. Parents had been asked to encourage their children to part from them at the school gate. Where they had attempted to take them into, or nearer to, the classroom, teachers had made it quite clear that this was not desirable. Some parents felt that the teachers needed to re-think their expectations and, in the words of one mother, "realize that not every child is going to be as adept or as quick as the next one, and to allow for this".

All the teachers interviewed recognized the importance of making contacts with parents, both prior to children's entry into school and at the time of entry. Staff in Lane End Infants School spoke of this period as "a crucial time" for undertaking "essential groundwork". Teachers stressed the importance of parents and teachers exchanging information and getting to know each other.

Some teachers had more ambitious expectations of these early contacts. In one instance, it was seen as a time for teachers to learn about children's backgrounds and note any problems, and for parents to "get both information about how the school runs and a description of how children will start to learn".

In Stanfield Middle School, which shared a site with the First School, the children had only to cross the playground to reach their new school, and the staff felt that the significance of the change was not apparent to parents. During the autumn term, the first of three evening meetings was held. Its purpose was to offer parents and teachers the opportunity to get to know each other. According to the deputy headteacher, these initial contacts were designed to "find out about a child's background, to discover which language is used at home, whether it is a happy home, what the needs and problems are and whether they are experiencing racism".

In Tatehill First School the purpose of the formal meeting for parents was said by the headteacher to be to make the all-important initial contact. It was also to introduce the idea of active cooperation in the preparation of their children for school. The headteacher was sure that most parents wanted to be involved in this but she did not think they knew how to go about it. Confidence, independence and self-discipline were the qualities which staff wanted parents to develop in their children rather than the skills of literacy or numeracy. One reception teacher was clear about what she did not want parents to do:

> I think far too many parents think that they have to teach them the alphabet and numbers... I want the children to be happy, confident, willing to try, counting nothing, reading nothing, not knowing that wretched alphabet. It's very hard to unteach anything that's been wrongly taught.

This attitude contrasts sharply with that of the headteacher of Lane End Infants School. She stressed the importance of parents and children enjoying their time together when very clear messages would be coming across to the child. These she identified as being:

> about love, care, concern and support. The parents are showing that they have a will to do good things with their child. It is the time together which is important even if parents are teaching nursery age children their tables.

Starting school at Tatehill First School

Meeting for parents before their children started school

About three months before their children were due to enter school, parents were invited to a meeting where they were given information about the school and shown a video made in the school. The Starting School packs were also introduced to parents. The majority of parents interviewed had attended this meeting and, with one exception, had all found it useful. They said that it had enabled them to see the way the school was organized and to meet the staff, as well as learn how they could prepare their children for school. The headteacher emphasized that it was a chance to make contact with parents, welcome them to the school and "show the parents that we are friendly and caring and would take good care of their children...to make it clear to them that they can come and chat to us, that we are not unapproachable. That was the most important part."

Starting School packs

All but one of the 13 parents interviewed had used at least one of the packs with their children and they were generally well received. A few parents did not think that their own children had learnt much from the packs, but conceded that they were good for those children who did not have access to the activities at home. Each pack includes a story book, a cassette, scissors and materials for developing skills needed in the reception class. Some parents thought that the packs had been a useful way of introducing tasks which would be done at school.

When parents were asked about specific items in the pack, the response was not so positive and they were unclear about the purpose of some of the activities and what their child should be gaining from them. Eight of them remembered using a counting activity from the pack, and although they said their children had enjoyed it, only one said that it was actually useful in terms of helping the child to count. Similarly, the parents who remembered using activities involving size and shape with their children reported that they were enjoyable but had not added to their children's existing knowledge of shapes. All the parents who had taken a pack had listened to the story tapes with their children, and most of them reported that their children had enjoyed listening to at least one of them, but it was not something new to any of them. In one case, the child thought they were too "babyish" and he did not want to listen to them. Initially, this had left his mother with a dilemma: "I felt obliged to make him listen to it but then I realized that he listened well to other things so I stopped making him."

Some of the parents who used the Starting School packs commented on the problems they encountered in getting into school to exchange them. These included having no transport at a particular time or having turned up on the wrong day and having to return on another occasion. A few parents commented on feeling awkward about bringing their younger children into school and on the practical difficulties which this sometimes involved. However, although there were reservations about the content of the packs and the practicalities of exchanging them, parents appreciated the part they played in providing a link between the home and school at this time. Indeed, one of the mothers talked in terms of them "bonding [my child] with the school".

The two reception teachers had different perceptions of the main purpose of the Starting School packs. One saw the link with the school as the most important aspect, so a child can say "'these have been given to me by my new school' regardless of what the activities are". The other teacher saw their purpose as helping to familiarize the child with school activities and expectations because she did not want a child "to throw a wobbly when faced with using a pair of scissors or a pencil; I want him to pick it up and try and have a bash". She went on to compare one little boy who had not had any packs with the other children who had started with him and had had the packs; she claimed that he "was the hardest to settle, and it was hardest for him to share me, he wanted my attention all the time. He was wild in the classroom on the first day...it [access to the packs] really makes a difference and this is how I can see it."

Both reception teachers were very positive about the benefits of the work on transition. One explained that "it saves me half a term getting to know the children", and both referred to what they called a "better level of skills" among the children who now came into school. While recognizing that it was not possible to associate this improvement solely with the use of packs, one of the teachers thought that hand control and attitudes to completing tasks were much better among children who had used them. The same teacher also referred to the "successful education of parents" and to their appreciation of being given guidance on "how to expand on reading activities, talking and playing games".

Children's contact with school prior to entry

As well as going with their parents to exchange the Starting School packs, the children were also invited to go into school for a lunch and for part of an afternoon. A few instances of tears and of not wanting to leave a parent's side were reported by their parents, but all those interviewed were enthusiastic about the opportunities which had been provided and about the influence these events had had in helping their children to settle happily in school. The teachers shared these feelings and spoke about the events with enthusiasm.

Meetings for parents after entry

Soon after the children started school, parents were invited to an evening meeting where teachers explained how English and maths were taught. Most children had been represented by one or both parents and all the parents who had attended thought it had been useful. While they were particularly appreciative of the opportunity to find out how their children were settling in, they also welcomed the chance to learn how these subjects were approached. One mother said it had made her "wish I was back at school; it was different and I liked that".

Teachers saw it as an opportunity to give parents confidence in, and knowledge of, the school and a chance to discuss individual children. They had longer-term perspectives than parents and could compare different intakes of children. On the basis of such comparisons, the headteacher reported that the meetings with parents were "more friendly now and pleasant and easier" and she related this improvement to the introduction of the Starting School packs. She commented that these parents had asked many more questions than their predecessors and felt that the relationship with parents had changed. She was firmly convinced of the effectiveness of the programme:

> Somehow the message was not getting through before. I told the parents all I could about starting school, but the children were not able to do what they are able to do now. The meetings were friendly, but we didn't achieve contact which was nearly so friendly or relaxed as it is now.

The transition to Overlea and Banthorpe Comprehensives

Soon after the start of the autumn term, most secondary schools begin to prepare for the pupils who will join them in the following September. The views of parents and of teachers were obtained on the meetings and other events held at this time in Overlea and in Banthorpe Comprehensive schools.

Meetings for prospective parents

As part of the induction programme, Overlea Comprehensive School held an open evening for prospective parents and pupils. There were also meetings in each of the six local primary schools. The open evening afforded the opportunity to hear about the school's approach and its general philosophy and see the facilities. The meetings in the primary schools allowed for more detailed information to be given on the curriculum and provided a further opportunity to ask questions. The teachers recognized that some parents felt that Overlea Comprehensive lacked the traditional underpinnings which some other schools in the area were seen to have. Rumours about poor standards of behaviour and academic results were known to circulate and these issues were brought into the open and fully discussed.

Nearly half of the parents who were interviewed had attended an open evening at Overlea, and even though they were recalling an event which had happened some 18 months earlier were positive about having had the opportunity to go into school and look round albeit out of normal hours. Most parents had also attended a meeting in their child's primary school. Most of those who had not been to such a meeting were either not living in the area at the time or had older children in the school, so they may have felt it was not necessary. Those parents who had attended had found it useful, although some could remember very little about what had been covered. There were some general comments such as "they showed slides of the school" and "told us about lessons and the examination results".

All the parents who had attended said that the areas of concern and interest to them had been covered, although some parents who had had prior contact with Overlea Comprehensive School said that they found it difficult to judge the meeting accurately because they knew so much about the school anyway. Others, however, remembered more about the meeting, because they *were* familiar with the school and it had added to what they already knew. Some parents said they had found the meeting of use precisely because it was their second time around, as is illustrated by one mother's experience, reported below. She had attended other meetings which the headteacher had addressed and believed that he did not really listen to what parents were asking:

> I did ask the head a question which was intended to get to how they would handle the kind of child who had disrupted my older son's first year... He misinterpreted the question totally. I tried to ask how long it took to assess the individual child and how the group worked as a whole with the teachers they came into contact with. He heard "assess" and went on to automatic about children with problems and how they can cater for these children. He missed my point, but having learnt by my experience, there is no way I'd let it happen again. But it is useful because forewarned is pre-armed...you are better informed second time around. I couldn't believe parents would miss meetings like these and that parents would sit there and say nothing. Second time around, you can hear things being said and with insight know what they mean when they say something.

Private visits to the school

Other studies have noted that parents who have been able to visit schools during working hours have valued the opportunity to see lessons and talk to members of staff in small groups (for example, Stillman and Maychell, 1986). The opportunity to make this kind of visit was available to parents in both second-ary schools. The acting headteacher at Overlea Comprehensive School estimated that about 40 families were shown around each year, but only one family interviewed had taken advantage of the offer. They telephoned the headteacher and explained that: "The next day we went to see the school. It was a day time – they are the best type [of visits] – you see the school in action, you see the work as well...we came away favourably impressed."

The other parents interviewed were aware that they could have made such a visit. One father explained his reasons for not going along: "On a one-to-one basis I think it could be in-timidating...the thing is that you always have the option to go in on your own but it is much easier to go in with a group of people…and on a one-to-one basis perhaps it would be glamorized."

School choice

It was clear that the majority of parents only seriously considered one secondary school at this time. Three-quarters of the Overlea parents had decided to send their children to the school before having the opportunity to attend any meeting (and all but one of these already had a child at the school). One-third of the parents could remember looking at the school's examination results, at this time, but no one claimed to have been influenced by them. They attached much importance to their children's preferences, as Petch (1986) found in her work. The belief that it was a caring school and the opinions of the primary school teachers also exerted strong influences on their decision. In some cases, a child's specific needs led a primary school teacher to recommend this school, as with this parent who was told that "there was good special needs help there and she [her daughter] had needed extra help at primary school". But in other cases, the advice seemed more idiosyncratic. One mother said that she had "talked to his teacher in the primary school. She said it was good enough for her son, so we thought it was good enough for us too." In fact a teacher in one of this school's local primary schools was also a parent in the sample. She had often discussed the respective merits of the local secondary schools with colleagues and she was shocked by the unfounded rumours which were spread. This had made her fearful of the advice they may have given to parents, as there seemed to be the idea that "nearly all the naughty children go there and all the well-behaved ones go somewhere else. Having worked in many schools on supply, including some of the so-called good ones, I'd say that was a load of nonsense."

Only one-quarter of the parents of children at Banthorpe Comprehensive had considered another school. Their reasons for opting for Banthorpe Comprehensive were wide-ranging and included looking for a school which provided a broad curriculum and good sporting activities; wanting a place at a school near to home; the preference of the child concerned; the continuity of the peer group; the existence of a well-regarded pastoral care system; and reasonable examination results.

Children's contact with the school

Many secondary schools have recognized the importance of contact with their future pupils before the actual time of entry. Senior staff of Banthorpe Comprehensive School visited all the local primary schools to meet the children who would be coming in September. The visit was seen as both a social event and a way of passing on information. This was followed by the pupils making a day-long visit to their new school. A similar day was arranged for the future pupils of Overlea Comprehensive School in the term prior to starting there. Parents appreciated the opportunities given to their children for contact with staff and pupils and the fact they could spend time in the school before an important move.

Parent's visits to the school before entry

Both secondary schools invited parents to an event in the term before their children started, but while there were common elements, the formats differed.

At Overlea Comprehensive School the children were invited into school for a full day and their parents for the afternoon. The headteacher and the first-year tutor talked to all of them about the first year, in particular, and more generally about the school, and a representative of the Parent–Teachers' Association (PTA) encouraged parents to be active in this body. The headteacher said he was sure that 80 per cent of a child's knowledge came from the parents and so urged them to work with the school for the good of the children. After the more formal meeting, they were all invited into classrooms to meet their children's personal tutors.

The vast majority of parents from Overlea knew that their children were going to this school, at this point, and most of them had attended the event. The ones who did not go along all had older children in the school, which may well have had an influence on their decision not to attend. Two mothers said they would have attended but were without a car in the daytime and there was no public transport in the afternoon.

Much of the information about the school's philosophy and the first-year timetable had already been given at other meetings, which may account for many parents being unable to recall specific areas covered. However, the parents who remembered most estimated that little had been achieved. One father said:

> Thinking back I got very little from it…the speeches didn't actually say a thing. It was waffle. I would like to be talked to in more concrete terms. I do think the head was an expert at 'blah'. It is common for teachers to speak to parents without saying much, and I did feel that was what happened.

Similarly, a mother who had taken time off work to attend did not feel that the meeting had been worthwhile. She had arrived late, "and I didn't know who was addressing the audience. I found out it was the head of the first year and I hadn't met her before; I felt I could have stayed at work because I'd heard it all before but it was also a lot of patter."

This mother had asked a question about how the weekly tutorial time, timetabled for the whole of one afternoon, was used and was dissatisfied with how the meeting had been conducted and how her question had been responded to:

> I was standing at the back and no one was saying anything, so I only asked it to break the ice. The teacher did not know anything about the school because she was new, but I knew enough to know that he [the head-teacher] hadn't answered it properly. It was a typical example of how not to organize something – it was not really thought out. He said, 'do ask anything you want to know', but in such a way to put parents off. He was intimidating…and the situation was intimidating.

Senior members of staff who were interviewed, and one of the tutors, were greatly enthusiastic about the parents' participation on this day. Other tutors, however, had found the question-time a stressful experience, particularly because they thought parents had been reluctant to ask questions. One of those teachers said: "I had never been so nervous in my life. I didn't know what to say and nobody had any questions." Another teacher, who had felt uncomfortable, said that he thought that parents had felt much the same because they had been brought together in a classroom, rather than put at their ease in a more informal venue with refreshments: "If parents have taken time off work to come to meet staff, what we do is just not good enough."

In Banthorpe Comprehensive, where the meeting for parents prior to their children starting school was held in the evening, part of the time was given to an address by the headteacher, who described the first-year curriculum and emphasized his "wish for a partnership between parents and the school" and the need for frequent contact to enable this to happen. As in Overlea Comprehensive, information was given on practical matters, such as uniform and transport, and the chairperson of the PTA addressed the parents. After these formal proceedings, parents and teachers met in a more relaxed atmosphere over coffee.

Most of the Banthorpe parents had attended this evening meeting and they all stated that they had found it useful. There was, however, a mixed response from the staff who were interviewed. The headteacher believed that the first part was a good opportunity to pass on information, even though it was rather long, because "there are things that had to be said and it is the only way to do it". One of the heads of House, while agreeing that a reinforcement from the platform would still be a good idea, thought that: "There is a point at which parents reach saturation point, when they get bombarded with information... Perhaps we could give out this information on paper and have them read it." However, they were all enthusiastic about the opportunity for more informal contact with parents. All three said that information about individual children was often conveyed to them at this stage and the form tutors were there if parents wished to speak to them.

The general intention among the staff for this part of the meeting was to allay any anxieties which parents might have at the thought of their children coming into a secondary school, which they knew could be seen as a frightening place.

Contacts between parents and staff after children's entry to secondary school

In Overlea Comprehensive School, the parents of new pupils were invited to a coffee evening soon after the term started. The idea for the evening had come from one of the tutors whose own parents had found schools intimidating places, and he wanted to show that teachers were approachable. More than half of the parents interviewed had attended and most of them welcomed the opportunity to put a name to a face (which many seemed to have forgotten from the first meeting the previous term) and obtain additional information on organization or additional items of uniform or stationery which should be obtained. Some parents had, however, found it unnecessary and rather a waste of time. As one mother said, "it was a little bit strained. She [the tutor] tried to make everyone feel at home but it is difficult. We didn't know anyone and it was just another awkward situation." And it was not only a feature of that particular tutor group. These parents had met the tutor whose idea the coffee evening had been and were left wondering what the point of it all had been: "He didn't know us and we didn't know him, and he didn't know our children. It was too early."

As far as the tutors were concerned, three out of the four appreciated this early contact with parents, although there was the feeling that parents expected them to deliver a talk. One tutor, who was less enthusiastic about the event than her colleagues, thought that parents might have been left wondering why they were there only to indulge in informal discussion and receive a little bit of information.

A few weeks after this coffee evening, the parents were invited to their first consultation session to discuss their children's progress with tutors. Again, there were some parents who did not understand why it had been held so soon after their children's entry. They had attended to hear how their children were progressing in their new school and tutors had not seemed to have anything to say to them. They had been left wondering why they had to attend, particularly as it was held during the day and they had had to rearrange other commitments.

A social and demonstration evening was held after the children had been at Banthorpe Comprehensive School for two months. In the past, each House had made its initial contact with parents in a different way. Some had held a social evening, which included some discussion of the curriculum, and others had organized individual sessions with the form teacher and head of House. Now they tried to combine both elements. As many staff as possible were there, and they were allocated time to make displays and prepare demonstrations which enabled parents to see and understand current teaching methods. There was time for parents to talk to teachers, and children were expected to introduce their parents to the head of House. All but two of the 17 families had attended this evening, and all but one of them said how much they had enjoyed it.

All three members of staff who were interviewed were extremely positive about these evenings and thought that parents would have found them of value. One said their strength lay in the fact that they were well thought out and "so there was a much better chance of conveying the message accurately". Another said that she would like to see them extended beyond the first year, so that "the children know the school is trying to build a relationship with the parents and that we are trying to work as a team. When we're working together, the child cannot play one off against the other."

Discussion

It was clear that parents and teachers appreciated the importance of these periods of transition and that schools took the opportunity to make contact with parents. Parents were generally positive about the way their children had settled into their new schools and about the efforts made by teachers to achieve this, as well as appreciating the ways in which they themselves had been involved. Until their children go to school, most parents have had no contact with the educational system since their own school days. It is not surprising therefore that parents wanted as much general explanation as possible, as well as more detailed information on their own children. What schools set out to achieve with parents was both ambitious and complex, highlighting the need for events to be organized to meet the purpose which they were supposed to serve. Although the schools were attempting to give parents information, they were not always providing the opportunities for parents to understand the reasons for certain practices. Similarly, teachers wanted to get to know parents and learn about their new pupils, but they had not always established the appropriate contacts to allow this to happen.

While a number of aims may be served by one meeting, it is essential for those planning the event to be clear about the priorities. It is possible to attempt too much at any one time and set too many goals for one encounter. Although some teachers wanted to learn about children's backgrounds, note any problems, provide parents with information about how the school ran and describe how their children would start to learn, it was doubtful that the opportunities provided for contact with parents would have allowed for anything as complex as their comments implied. Some of the teachers also referred to learning from parents about the children's backgrounds and any family or personal problems, but no one raised the issue of how parents would feel about opening up to strangers or how they would feel about teachers wanting to know if they had a 'happy home'.

It is also important that parents should not be left wondering why they have been invited into school. Parents and teachers recalled meetings and sessions which had served little purpose. A member of the research team attended one meeting for parents of new entrants where most of the time was given to reading out sections of the school booklet and going through a list of dos and don'ts, most of which were contained in the newsletter which was distributed. There is the danger that meetings which are bland and uninformative will put parents off. Where this is combined with people feeling uncomfortable in schools, it is perhaps not surprising that some parents do not come back.

Parents cannot be expected to understand how a school operates or why the curriculum is structured in a particular way after one brief meeting. Neither should they be expected automatically to understand and accept why particular rules are imposed or certain activities adopted. The parents of children in the reception class in Tatehill First School who were unhappy about putting them on the school bus from day two had not found it easy to take this up with the school. It is difficult for parents unfamiliar with a school to question practices which they are unhappy about when they appear to be accepted as norms by other parents. They need the opportunity to ask questions away from the potentially constraining atmosphere of a large meeting, and to find out more about the school's policies, practices and philosophy.

It is clear that the perspectives of professionals and of parents will not always coincide, particularly at a time when they are new to each other. One way of dealing with this is to encourage the daytime visits which were available in both secondary schools. But invitations alone are inadequate; consideration needs to be given to alternative forms of organization. Again, parents may find it less intimidating to go round in a small group where they still have the opportunity to ask questions without the pressures they might feel in a large meeting.

The acting headteacher of Overlea Comprehensive School was concerned about the questions which parents did not ask and about the rumours which were never brought out into the open. It is possible that a large meeting intended to convey information to parents was not an appropriate event at which to draw this out. Much may have remained unsaid because there was not an appropriate medium for dialogue. Parents might have had the opportunity to raise their concerns, had this been a specific aim of the meeting. The school would also have been able to counter misleading information and "unfounded rumours" stemming from some schools which Overlea regarded as "partners".

There will always be decisions which are based on instinct or hearsay. As far as the choice of secondary schools was concerned, it was apparent that a great deal of importance was placed on the children's own preferences. This study further confirms Johnson and Ransom's (1983) findings, that most parents make a decision on the basis of 'circumstances prevailing at the time of transfer, rather than with an eye to the ensuing five or seven years'. Nevertheless, it is still important for schools to give parents the opportunities to ask questions when they want to and provide them with sufficient information of the kind they would value at this time of change.

The efforts made by schools to increase the confidence of parents to approach them may be seriously undermined if parents are made to feel, just as their children go into school, that they have been "doing it all wrong" in relation to the teachers' expectations. Teachers in Lane End Infants and Tatehill First School had very different ideas about what parents should do with their children before they come into school at five. In one school, one of the reception teachers did not want parents to attempt to 'teach' their children; and in another, the headteacher favoured any parental input and regarded it as a positive sign that they wanted to be involved. This is just one potential area of difficulty which has to be negotiated: a parent has the right to decide which activities to engage in with a pre-school child but is not usually in a position to judge how these will be received by a school.

The Starting School packs were professionally produced, attractive resources, and while they were not evaluated in this study, the comments of teachers and parents provided some insights into how they were perceived and used.

The reception class teachers referred to the skills children had acquired from using the packs, and one of them referred to the new ideas and concepts they had introduced to parents. Parents saw this quite differently: most of them appreciated the activities as additional material, rather than because they changed what they were already doing with their children. They were happy with the way their children had settled into school and valued the concrete way in which packs provided a link between home and school.

The judgement which was made by a teacher in Tatehill School about the child who had not had access to an activity pack and who had not settled when he was admitted to school raised an important issue. In this instance, although the parents of the child expressed very positive attitudes towards the school and its staff when they were interviewed, they had not really seen the point of the packs. They had not been at the initial meeting where the packs had been introduced and, despite the fact that they had older children in the school, the teachers were opposed to sending the packs home because they wanted all the parents to come into school. There is no evidence necessarily linking the child's difficult start in school to his not having had the packs, but if the school believed in a connection it was in their power to make contact with the home. Again, it suggests how important it is for schools to be clear about the reasons for initiating these activities and then to establish the appropriate means of ensuring they are able to meet their objectives.

The responsibility for initiating contact with parents at this time lies with teachers. Meetings and other events have to be sufficiently interesting and informative to make parents want to come again. This means that teachers have to think about why they are bringing parents in and what can be said in a meeting that cannot be conveyed by other means. Some parents find schools intimidating places and they have many other demands on their time. If meetings are used constructively; if efforts are made to make parents and teachers feel at ease with one another; and if a sufficiently supportive attitude exists so as not to make parents feel that they have failed before they have come into the school, a good foundation for future contact will have been laid.

6 Home Visiting and Other Services

Introduction

One frequently mentioned reason for embarking on work with parents is to link the two major parts of a child's life – the home and the school. As one way of achieving this, some teachers make home visits, on a regular basis, to work with parents and children and others visit to help parents understand more about their children's schools.

The views of parents and teachers on home visiting are presented in the early part of this chapter and they are followed by the data from three places where initiatives, based on home visiting, were established. The first of these was concerned with the work of an educational home visitor (EHV) attached to Dalebridge Nursery School; the second was in Stanfield Middle School where the visits were part of its approach to reading; and the third was Newborough's Early Years Support Team.

Home visiting

Both the Plowden (1967) and Bullock (1975) Reports supported the practice of home visiting, but the evidence from the headteachers' questionnaire in this study indicated that it had been introduced as a regular feature in only one-quarter of all schools and that it was far more common in nursery schools (45 per cent of respondents) and in special schools (65 per cent). In other countries, notably the USA, there have been large-scale intervention programmes where home visiting has been an integral part, for instance, Project Home Start (see Bache and Nauta, 1979). There are examples of similar projects

in the UK, many focusing on young children with special educational needs (for example, Cameron, 1982).

Some nursery and reception teachers visit the homes of children about to enter school to establish early contact with
parents and obtain a fuller picture of the child. Similar initiatives with children at other stages in their school careers do
occur but are less common. The dominant pattern still is for
parents and teachers to meet only on school premises.

Views on home visiting

A substantial majority of parents (nearly four-fifths) were either
wholly in favour of home visiting or in favour but with some
reservations. However, it is interesting to consider the value
attached to such visits by parents who had actually recieved
them, as well as the views of those who had not. Nearly one-
third of interviewed parents had received at least one visit. This
was a higher percentage than would be expected from a ran-
dom sample of parents because the group was drawn from
schools some of which had been selected because home visiting
was a feature of their current practice.

There was a greater level of support for the idea among
parents who had received a visit, with the majority being in
favour of this practice and the rest being in favour with some
reservations. Most of these visits were made in connection with
the initiatives described later in this chapter; others were either
in response to a specific problem, or were part of a home–
school reading initiative in a secondary school or undertaken
routinely for children about to start primary school.

Where there had been a problem, parents greatly appreciated
this type of contact with staff. One mother, whose eldest son
had recently left school, said that he had never enjoyed his time
there and had always rebelled against it, but she was full of
praise for the support she had received from staff: "At least
three teachers regularly visited the home because he had such
problems. Then, when my daughter was bullied and ran away
from school, the deputy came around on the same day and was
very supportive and kind." While she thought many people
might find the idea of such visits intimidating, they had in fact
provided the opportunity to talk freely about problems, in an
environment where she had felt more confident. This was a

point made by a number of other parents who had received visits in similar circumstances.

The seven parents who had taken part in the shared reading project, discussed in Chapter 3, received a home visit as part of it. All had been happy to be visited and, with one exception, were extremely positive about the event. However, two expressed some reservations about the practice if it was used more generally. The parents who viewed home visits most positively appreciated the opportunity for teachers to gain another perspective on their pupils by seeing them in the home setting, where the parents themselves found it easier to talk.

In contrast to this, however, were the views of a group of parents who had been visited by a teacher before their children started at the primary school in Planeborough, all of whom expressed reservations. They did not find them useful and thought that they should only be made when there was a problem. They could remember little about the visit, describing it as somewhat low key and general and, were they to be used routinely, wanted to see the introduction of a more structured approach.

Of the parents who had not experienced a home visit, the majority were willing to welcome a teacher into their homes. It was felt that home visits would show that a school cared about every pupil, enable teachers to see children in their home environment and provide a good opportunity for informal discussion. There were also those parents who said they would appreciate a visit but were unable to say why. Only a small number saw visits as a way of solving their own practical problems of finding a babysitter or taking time off work in order to go to their children's school.

There were parents who were uncertain of the value of home visits, including nearly one-fifth who expressed some reservations; most of these did not see any value in a general policy of home visiting and wanted teachers to go into homes only when the need arose. There were some parents who commented on the personal qualities required of teachers making the visits and on the importance of respecting parental territory. Such qualities would be those which enabled them to create a relaxed atmosphere and yet maintain professionalism in relation to what was discussed. Their remit should be restricted to school work and should not include anything which could be perceived as being "nosey".

Over one-fifth of parents opposed home visits under any circumstances. Most of them could see no purpose because they felt able to approach the school at any time and were happy to do so. There were, however, a small number of parents who said they would find a home visit both an intrusion and an imposition, including one father who felt that it also placed an unnecessary burden on teachers:

> Teachers have come in for a lot of stick over the past few years, and in my opinion much of it has been fully justified, but they are entitled to a private life themselves. I also think that a line has to be drawn between the teacher and the pupils... I think a child's private life has to be respected as well. Too close a tie between the home and the school may not serve the child well.

More than two-thirds of teachers were in favour of home visiting. A few had reservations and the remaining quarter were against the idea. It was difficult to obtain an accurate picture of the home visiting undertaken by these teachers. Many said that they had visited parents in the past, and even teachers who were against the idea in principle had made a visit in response to a specific problem or difficulty. It was, however, possible to say that one-sixth were regularly going into the homes of pupils, and many teachers who were not doing so, or had never made a home visit, held positive views about their value.

There was a distinction between those teachers who viewed visits as essential, or at least a very important contribution to their work, and those who considered that home visits had a more limited role. In the former category were the members of the Stileborough Parental Involvement Team. One aspect of their work was a Homestart programme which they took out into homes. They usually worked with families where older children had already entered school, and class teachers thought that younger siblings at home would benefit from the programme. A member of the team was very clear about the value of home visiting right across the age range:

> I think home visiting is absolutely vital in some areas and there is no substitute for it. No matter how much empathy a classroom teacher has with individual children, it is very difficult to really know the background of the child and

cater for its needs without knowing the family. A ten-minute home visit can have far-reaching effects in the way you see the child's needs and go to meet them. I feel that very strongly from personal experience. I know there is a point of view that sees home visits as intrusive. I can see that could be the case. I believe people who make them need certain skills, some people naturally have them, some can have the skills developed and I think there is probably a minority of people who should never make them.

There were other teachers who, while they did not make as many visits as members of the Stileborough team, had built such contact into their work and used home visiting for different purposes. A number of teachers had used visits as a means of contacting parents who did not come into schools, and their potential in this respect was recognized even by teachers who had never been into pupils' homes. This point was emphasized by two senior teachers in different comprehensive schools. One said that, "if you want to build up relationships there must be an alternative for those who don't come into school. You are duty-bound to follow them up."

There was widespread acknowledgement that not all teachers would be able to undertake home visiting, and some said that they would only be willing to undertake this after training and with the help and support of senior staff. It was generally felt that teachers should never automatically be expected to make visits.

One teacher pointed out that there was always the possibility that "unless handled carefully, parents could think you are prying when entering their homes". In fact teachers admitted to learning a considerable amount about home backgrounds during the visits. One teacher said that such contacts were vital because "some children are going through experiences that many of us can't imagine".

In Overlea Comprehensive School, home visiting was not actively encouraged, although tutors were not prevented from making them. The acting headteacher supported one teaching union's caution against home visiting, but he nevertheless valued these contacts because they provided "a mutuality with parents on their own terms" and showed that:

> we are willing to be put out and that we care...it is an education for many teachers, and they need to move from seeing the world in a one-dimensional way, for example, to see poverty and affluence...I have done some myself and it is humbling to realize the great significance for families, more than ought to be.

Even when the primary purposes of the visits were said to be "to build relationships" and "make contact with parents", teachers sometimes introduced other aims. In the primary school in Planeborough visits were made to the homes of all children about to start in the nursery, and a teacher referred to their role in relation to the assessment of the child. A letter was sent to all parents suggesting a day when a teacher might call to meet them and the child. Although the teacher who made these visits said it was important "to reassure mum that we know what she is concerned about", she saw it as an easy way to make the first assessment because the atmosphere was usually relaxed.

For those teachers for whom it was an integral part of their work, home visiting was built into their timetables. Otherwise any commitment to home visiting raised the question of when it was done and how it was managed. Whether the home visits were made in the day or in the evening, special arrangements were required. Overlea Comprehensive, where the shared reading project was based, provided time off in lieu for the teachers, to compensate for the evenings given over to visiting homes, but staff were unwilling to disrupt their pupils' lessons to take advantage of this.

Teachers who were not in favour of home visiting comprised those who were categorically opposed to the principle and those who did not think it would contribute to their work. Although they were equally divided between the primary and secondary sectors, those in the primary schools for the most part said they could see no value in the exercise, while secondary teachers tended to have more definite reasons for not wanting to go into pupils' homes. Some teachers felt that they did not have the confidence and felt happier to talk with parents in school. Others thought they lacked other necessary skills, such as counselling, to make visits routinely and to be of help to parents. In addition, there was a fairly frequent comment that visits would probably have to be made in their own time without any compensation for petrol used or free time lost.

A few teachers believed that there was something intrinsically wrong with these visits. Usually this meant they were viewed as intrusive and unnecessary. The strongest statements against home visiting came from some members of the staff in Marksbury Comprehensive School, although elements of what was said were expressed by a few teachers in other schools. Despite the enthusiasm of the deputy headteacher for home visits, they were rarely made and some teachers voiced considerable antipathy towards them. The senior teacher, who had responsibility for home–school relations, attached some theoretical value to them, but this was outweighed by his fears as a parent of being on the receiving end and "meeting a fresh-faced probationer on the doorstep who said, 'I teach your children and I am here to tell you all about them'".

Home visiting and pre-nursery groups in Dalebridge Nursery School

Home visiting

All the Dalebridge parents who were interviewed had received at least one home visit; some had older children and had received more. They were all very positive about the experience, especially about the approachability and warmth of the educational home visitor. In fact the only negative comment was made by a mother referring to a visit which had been made when her older child was registered for a nursery place. She regarded that one as "a waste of time" – as she did any such visit, unless "there is something wrong with the child or the child is special". Most parents, however, valued the opportunity to discuss the nursery in general and, in some cases, welcomed the chance to discuss specific problems they were experiencing.

The headteacher and the EHV stressed the value of the visits as part of the school's policy of establishing a warm, friendly relationship with parents from the start. Yet there were noticeable differences in emphasis. The EHV said she thought that "all families appreciate the interest in the child" and the commitment this shows. She had been surprised by the level of concerns which she had found even in families without obvious problems. The headteacher drew attention to the information which the school obtained during these visits, saying that "we can see how conditions are and how the parents react to each other".

As well as establishing early liaison with the home, the headteacher referred to a screening purpose in the visits to identify those families who might need support. This was not mentioned by the EHV, although she selected families for the pre-nursery groups during the visits and recorded information about families on a form. This was attached to the admission form and could therefore be accessed by members of staff. When parents were asked to check the children's application forms, the sheets containing any comments made by the EHV were removed. The EHV thought that parents were sometimes perplexed by the visits and viewed them as a form of assessment, although no such feelings were expressed by the parents who were interviewed.

The pre-nursery groups

The parents could all remember being told about the group in the course of their home visit, and some recalled how it had been presented as an opportunity for their children to be eased into school, which had seemed to be a good idea. Other parents said that the group had been promoted as a means of helping the children with regard to their shyness, developmental delay or 'giftedness'. One mother had been attending the group for some time but was still unaware that not all pre-nursery children were offered a place in a group and that there had been some selection. In fact two other mothers said that they did not realize until they attended, that the group was for children with 'problems'.

All the mothers thought that their children had gained from attending a group and had thoroughly enjoyed going. The benefits were seen in terms of learning to share and mix with peers and enjoying activities such as painting and drawing, although one mother said her son's interest in these had disappeared after two months and he had made no particular progress. Another mother was pleased to be able to take her child to school, so that he became familiar with the environment from an early age.

The mothers had all found the groups pleasant and friendly, and a few were very enthusiastic about the enjoyment they gained from attending. Two-thirds referred to positive outcomes from their attendance. These included an improvement in their confidence in managing their children, an introduction to particular activities which the children enjoyed and access to sources of support for themselves. Most wanted to meet more frequently, one would have preferred a longer session than the one and a half hours provided, and one wanted to have the option of leaving the children. One mother thought that two teachers were needed because of the demands made by mothers *and* children, and another that the children should be grouped on the basis of their needs, so that appropriate therapies could be introduced. Another mother was critical of people who came along and failed ever to make the drinks and tidy up. But a more serious criticism was of the lack of a "middle ground" for children who were not yet in nursery or were not going to go, but did not have problems.

While both the EHV and the headteacher agreed that one of the main aims of the home visit was to 'select' the families it was judged would benefit from the pre-nursery group, they differed about the purpose of these groups. The EHV viewed them as a preparation for nursery school and emphasized the opportunities for children to mix, for the teacher to assess any particular needs children may have and for the mothers to "enjoy the child". In contrast, the headteacher said that they were "not preparing the children for nursery school, although the parents might think this". As was noted earlier, the evidence from the interviews with parents indicated that indeed they thought just that.

The members of staff agreed on the criteria for selection and on the main focus of activity in the groups. The EHV, who had been in post for just under a year, had been happy to accept the rules-of-thumb which she had inherited from her predecessor. In the first place, it seemed to be that priority should be given to children who had English as a second language and those who did not go to a playgroup. Other factors for selection were isolation; a child who was shy or clinging; and those with specific difficulties, including behaviour problems. She went on to say that the groups were a "meeting place for mothers who may be isolated and without friends", for those who could not face going to parent-and-toddler groups.

The EHV viewed her position as quite complex, and there were occasions when she was not sure how to balance her time. She referred to the run-up to Christmas when a lot of personal problems had been exposed and she felt that she had given 95 per cent of her time to the mothers and actually very little to the children. At other times, the balance had been quite different. She said she tried unobtrusively to suggest to the parents ways of dealing with children, but was forever conscious that she did not want to intervene in a direct way; and neither was she in a position to change the attitudes of people who had not come along to be lectured to.

The headteacher saw the groups as providing some form of compensation for a deficiency in the home, and focused on the benefits of the 'educational stimulation' the children received. However, as already mentioned, the EHV regarded the groups as a preparation for nursery and an opportunity for the children to mix. Both she and the headteacher were in agreement about the benefits to the parents, which were seen to be both social and practical, in so far as they were given help to "cope with behaviour problems, feeding, toilet-training and sleep". Most of the disadvantages might apply to any group, such as when they fail to gel or to accept all members.

Home visiting and a video in Stanfield Middle School

A system of home visiting in this school had been in operation for four years and the headteacher estimated that each year approximately four-fifths of the parents of first-year children were visited. A video had been made to show parents how crucial reading was and how they could share books with their children. The emphasis was on the importance of reading to life, inside and outside school, and how both teachers and parents, even if they did not speak the same language, could work together with the child. It was intended that a copy of the video should be left with each family when the home visit was made. This did sometimes happen but during the periods when such visits were observed it was equally likely that copies would not be available to take out on visits or the teacher concerned forgot to take them with her, or having taken them, forgot to leave them in the homes.* Of the parents of first-year children who were interviewed, only half had seen the video and one of these had seen it at an open evening in the school. Of those who had viewed it at home, some reported that their children, not the teacher, had delivered it to them.

Most parents had been contacted about a teacher visiting their home and they all said they would welcome such a visit, although only just over half had received one. There was a variety of reasons for this. Sometimes the parents said they had returned the form to the school saying what time would be convenient for a teacher to call but they had heard nothing more. Other parents had found it difficult to find time to see a teacher and, in one instance, an appointment had not been kept by the teacher and no further contact had been made with the family.

The focus of the home visit was on involving parents in their children's reading, and all the parents who had met a teacher in their home remembered a discussion of books and of reading; comments were made, such as: "I found out more about reading to my children, to listen to them and question them after I have been reading." A few parents remembered a more general discussion as well, usually covering a child's general progress and behaviour in school. The visits were said to have lasted between five minutes and half an hour and the overall impression was that they had been useful.

All but one of the parents who had seen the video had found it of value. Parents said that they had learnt how they could help their children and, while it was seen to cover much the same ground as the home visit, it had the advantage of showing them how they could use Punjabi or Urdu when reading with their children.

The headteacher explained that these visits had been introduced at a time when the school was revising its language policy and wanted to involve parents more actively in sharing books with their children. He identified four purposes for the visits. First, they were intended to reach out and say to parents that the school believed that they had an important role to play in their children's education. Secondly, they were seen as a direct point of contact for those parents who were unable to go into school, and thirdly, as a vehicle for alerting parents to the

* It should be noted that there was a video recorder in every home that was visited by the researcher and the teacher concerned said she had never been told that a machine was not available in a home.

role they played in helping children's language development. Their final, vital purpose was "to open up the school, which was part of the indigenous culture, and help to break down the barriers which had separated the home and the school".

The teacher who undertook the visits during the period of the study thought that because many of the parents had been educated abroad in systems which had emphasized rote learning, this had left them with a "very unimaginative approach to education" which she considered had to be changed. One of her main tasks was to show them how much assistance they could give by just talking to their children and interacting on a one-to-one basis. Often she felt parents did not understand how narrow their children's vocabulary was and, in turn, how this limited their depth of understanding.

The teacher was concerned that parents were not always aware that their children were having problems: "so long as they can speak English, they assume all is well. Parents sometimes do not understand that the children need to understand what they read." This teacher appreciated that some teachers felt nervous at the prospect of meeting parents out of school and had fears about having to cope with parental anger or resentment. Such anxieties were, she thought, largely unfounded. What she had experienced was an overwhelming enthusiasm from parents for home visits, which had led to a belief in their worth.

The three form teachers expressed no such reservations and supported the visits because they thought they had real advantages. All believed that subsequent contact in school with the parents involved had been made much easier. None of the teachers had seen language as a problem, even though they did not speak the community languages used in the homes they visited. The teacher who had made most of the visits said: "If parents appear to have a problem understanding what I am saying I simplify it; often families bring in a relative to act as a translator, and I've only once needed to take an interpreter."

The only criticism made by the form teachers related to the time allocated for home visiting. In previous years, they had made a few visits in their own time, but more recently, the multicultural support service teacher had been allocated two afternoons and one morning period in which to complete them. Although she said she would prefer to share the task or hand it over completely to class teachers, she thought that her colleagues did not want to leave their classes during the day or visit outside school hours. Her opinion was that even though their commitment to the visits had increased, it was hard to expect people to do them after school, particularly since the introduction of directed time. She herself used to make visits late into the evening to fit in with parents' worktime, but she now firmly drew the line at 3.30 pm. Nevertheless, she did not like being out of school during the day because she felt she left the burden of teaching on her colleagues. It was not clear, however, how much this had been discussed between the teachers.

Two teachers interviewed in this school had never made a home visit, and while one expressed reservations the other was opposed to the notion. This teacher felt that they were "unacceptably intrusive"; the other said she approved of the idea, but as a member of the Asian community, she was concerned about how the visits appeared to parents. She said that, while not referring specifically to the teacher who had made the visits, a white perspective could have led teachers to enter homes with preconceived ideas and it was important not to be judgemental.

When the teachers were asked for their opinion about the video, their reactions were generally favourable. The teacher who was principally responsible for the home visits had made the video with an advisory teacher. She said that she had received only positive comments from parents, although she felt that they regarded it as "no more than a nice thing for a school to have done" and had not thought beyond that. The headteacher and some other members of staff were very enthusiastic about the video, although the former did say that he had hoped it would have had a commentary in Punjabi, and plans were in hand to correct this.

The only note of dissatisfaction came from a member of the teaching staff, who said that she had been left feeling "uncomfortable...as an Asian, I felt we were treated as if we were backward. I didn't like the tone of the questioning. The hidden ethos made me uncomfortable."

The toy and book libraries for pre-school children

Parents who attended the pre-nursery group in Dalebridge Nursery School had access to toy and book libraries. So did the parents who had attended similar groups in a primary school in Planeborough, but only two of these 13 parents remembered using the scheme. One mother had borrowed books, toys and jigsaws, but only on two occasions at the most; and the other had borrowed toys regularly but not until later, when her child had entered the nursery. Although two parents said they had not been aware that they could borrow anything, the majority of those interviewed did not think they needed the library and would have preferred to buy.

Of the mothers who attended the Dalebridge pre-nursery group, one-half said they regularly used the toy library and rather more used the book library. The toy library was valued by two mothers, in particular, because it allowed them to try out toys before buying them and to borrow toys which they would not consider buying. A mother who used the book library regularly said she did so to encourage a sense of responsibility in her son, who did look after and enjoy the books which he had borrowed. The only other comment from a regular user of this provision was not so positive: she allowed her child to take books home because he was keen, but she did not regard it as necessary because they had lots of books and used the public library.

A substantial proportion of parents had chosen not to use either of the libraries. From the five who did not use the toy library, the feeling was that the toys on offer were of little interest. Their children had toys of thier own that were similar to some of those on offer. One mother added that it was just making work to try to keep the toys unspoilt for a week; and similar reasons were proffered by the four mothers who did not use the book library.

As for the teachers in Planeborough school, one thought that the initial years of the book and toy library for the very young children had been greeted with much enthusiasm, until financial problems had forced closure. Another member of staff had felt that "those who need it wouldn't come in here, or if they did, pride would prevent them asking". In view of this, there were plans to take toys and books out into the community in the school's mini-bus once additional funding was available for re-starting the scheme. It was less clear how another pitfall mentioned by a different member of staff was to be avoided: "At first there was enthusiasm from both parents and teachers.

But it's always the same, the teachers become jaded, the parents think that's the end [of it], so it becomes counter-productive."

Both teachers associated with the pre-nursery groups in Dalebridge Nursery School had similar reservations about their toy library, although the majority of parents were said to use the book library weekly and it was described as an "excellent facility". The headteacher was conscious of wanting to educate parents and "to help those whose only example of toys are the adverts on television", which frequently represented violence rather than being "more imaginative". However, making parents aware of other toys only seemed to work well when items were new, which indicated the need to provide money to maintain the toys to a high standard. The EHV made the same point, and echoed the view of the teacher in the other school when she said she had sometimes been aware of a feeling that to borrow toys implied an inability to buy them.

The work of the Newborough Early Years Support Team with families of young children with special educational needs

The initial contact

All of the parents in the Newborough sample reported feelings of gratitude or relief when a member of the team first visited them at home. In some cases, a condition or disability had been diagnosed at birth or during the early months of a child's life. Reactions which were reported at the diagnosis included feelings of failure; of panic; of mourning for what might have been; and of isolation. Other parents had suspected that something was wrong with their child soon after the birth and had to wait – and occasionally 'put pressure on' – for this to be confirmed and diagnosed. Both sets of parents included many who had not known of the team's existence and who were relieved to find out that support was available.

The visits

Many mothers said that it had been stressed that it was up to them whether they took part or not and that, once they had decided to participate, the initial visit from the teacher who was going to work with the child occurred within a few weeks. Parents commented on the confidence they had gained as they watched their children learn new skills through play and engage in activities which they were then able to use. Parents had been told in the past to stimulate their children as much as possible, but they had not always been sure that they were doing the right thing. They valued the opportunity of having an experienced teacher in their home whom they could watch working with their children.

There were many references to particular skills which the children had learnt from the home teachers, often when other attempts to teach the same things had failed. However, in order to carry on with the work started during the visit, parents sometimes had to learn more than how to teach the skill on which the teacher had been concentrating. One mother of a boy severely disabled by cerebral palsy was pleased that he was being taught to hold a cup and spoon and to sort shapes and stack cups, to match colours and to play games, but the crucial aspect for her was that, "she [the teacher] has taught me how to *approach* different things like puzzles, how to make him do *something* before letting him go off " (mother's emphases).

The week's programme

Most parents said they worked with their children every day on the tasks that had been agreed with the teachers. In some cases, the week's programme might comprise no more than a few ideas suggested by the teacher, but the mothers took these just as seriously as more structured plans.

Even though most parents were keen to work with their children, they did not always find it easy. Their children would do things for the teacher which they would not do for them. However, the teachers assured them that the difficulties which they faced were not unusual, and sometimes they were able to work out appropriate strategies together.

There were some parents who were unable to work with their children; for example, this mother:

> What Carolyn has done has been a tremendous help for getting her ready for nursery. There wasn't anything I could not do if I had the patience. When Carolyn is here, it is just the two of us with her; but when I do it, the

> other children are calling for my attention all the time.
> Carolyn does leave two or three tasks to be practised and I
> tell her truthfully what I have done. Anyway she can see if
> I have done anything with Claire because if I have she is
> better at it.

In exceptional cases, the team had decided that they would be
involved with families, even though the parents were unlikely
to work with the children; for example, there was one family
where both children had full-time nursery places and, although
a member of the team visited the home regularly, the mother
was not aware that she was expected to do anything with her
sons between visits.

Only one parent expressed any reservations about the
activities which were left for her daughter each week. This
mother said that she worked "intensively" with the child every
day and did not think that the teacher pushed her enough.
Although she admitted doing "more and more advanced
activities" than the ones which were suggested, she had never
discussed it with the teacher.

The value of contact

Despite the possible pitfalls, all the parents interviewed reported
that their contact with the team had been useful and that they
had gained from it, as had their children. The reassurance and
support was greatly appreciated and helped boost self-
confidence. One mother valued the knowledge that "someone
will come in regularly. I find it useful to have someone there to
tell you that you are doing the right thing; it would be all too
easy to leave him lying on the floor."

Many parents were able to point to how their children had
learnt specific tasks. But one of the most valued aspects of their
contact with the team was the advice and help given to parents
when their children were about to enter school. This comment
was one of many which referred to the way the team's advice
and experience had allowed parents to stand back and think
about their children's future, before they made an informed
decision about what they wanted:

> She guided me in a lot of ways. I did not know about
> integration. I would have found a private place for her.

Pam has also taught me not to plan ahead, to take it a day at a time with my daughter. She stopped me making a mistake about schools and I don't know who we would have turned to without this team for advice.

Parents' role in relation to the team

The majority of parents wanted to work with the team to help their children to learn, although the range of responses reflected the confidence that these parents had in their own ability to teach their children. Some parents saw it as part of their responsibility and would have embarked on plans of their own, but nevertheless valued the informed assistance of the team. Other parents did not think they would have known where to start.

Most of the parents were enthusiastic about their involvement and, while they appreciated the contact their children had with other professionals, such as a speech therapist or physio-therapist, the team was seen as in some way 'special'. Working alongside the teacher gave them the confidence to go on teaching their children between visits and this was a much-valued aspect of the service. This contrasts with what Dale (1986) found in her study of the parents of pre-school children involved in a similar home-based service. What that group of parents valued, more than their own involvement in the programme, was having an experienced teacher in their home; and many of them would in fact have preferred to have left any intervention entirely to a teacher. This is not to say that similar feelings were not reported at all in the present study. A few mothers were not as enthusiastic about their own contributions, and two were opposed to the idea of teaching their own children – but that was very much a minority view.

The report and review procedure

One of the main duties of this team was to assess the children's possible special educational needs, based on the information gathered over a period of time, and to provide the education department with this information. Allied to this was their responsibility to provide information to parents about the range of provision in the authority and the procedures to gain admission to such provision. The assessment was based on the model of continuous teaching intervention in the child's home and led to a detailed report presented to an informal educational assessment review meeting. This 'report' was in fact a series of reports written by the key people involved with the child, including the parents.

Nearly one-half of the families had already been through the report and review procedure, and nearly half that group had contributed a report on their child. They all mentioned the guidelines for the report which had been given to them by their visiting teachers, and the discussions with these teachers which took place before they were written.

It was usual for the head of the pre-school service to attend the review meeting together with the parents, the teacher who had worked with the child, the senior clinical medical officer, an educational psychologist and any other professionals who had been involved with the child; speech therapists and health visitors too were often present. Most of those parents who had been through the review procedure were very satisfied with the way the meeting had gone and with the outcome. Those who were not so satisfied were not critical of the teachers on the team but of the contributions of the other professionals who had been involved.

One mother had been extremely surprised to discover that the head of the nursery which her son attended considered him to be "uncooperative" and in danger of being "swallowed up in a reception class" of a mainstream school. Nevertheless, she was willing to accept the headteacher's recommendation that the child would benefit from attending a special unit because it was based on a long-term assessment of his ability and his potential. What had made her angry was the apparent speed with which the educational psychologist had dealt with the nursery visit and the review. She was critical of the fact that he had not only 'dismissed' her child on the basis of a 20-minute visit to the class, but also left the review meeting before the end. She viewed this apparent lack of commitment as effectively undermining the work she and others had done with her son: "It is almost as if all the time you are working towards the review and you need to feel it went well and I came out feeling annoyed and disappointed."

Another mother, who had tried to get her child into a mainstream nursery school, felt that the doctors had an insufficient commitment to the principle of integration. She believed that if they had really been in favour of it, the others involved in the decision-making process would have been unable to resist their arguments. As the situation stood, she saw herself and the team as "out on a limb" pushing against the status quo.

Despite these criticisms, it was clear that the parents valued their involvement in this review process. There was certainly an element of viewing themselves as working alongside the team to counter-balance any misjudgement by other professionals, even though this was not always successful.

Discussion

Most parents and teachers indicated that they were in favour of home visiting, whether or not they had experience of this sort of contact. The parents thought that home visiting indicated that a school cared and genuinely wanted to communicate with them. This belief was shared by many teachers, who thought that the contacts helped to build relationships with parents and break down some of the barriers, to open up communication between the school and home and, at the same time, show that they cared for the pupils' overall welfare. But even among the parents who valued visits from teachers very highly, there was no evidence to support the proposition made by Overlea Comprehensive School's acting headteacher that they regarded them, in any way, as a privilege.

The fact that some teachers pointed to the positive changes in the nature of their relationship with parents after contacting them at home indicates the dynamics which are involved. Teachers were conscious that their presence could be interpreted as an intrusion, although very few parents raised this as an issue. What was of more concern to parents was that teachers made clear the purpose of their visits. In fact the only parents to express any dissatisfaction with visits that they had received criticized the teachers' lack of focus when they had called.

Visits to homes give teachers the opportunity to learn a great deal about their pupils' backgrounds – but also pose some dilemmas. For instance, how can a balance be achieved between maintaining confidentiality and providing colleagues with appropriate information? This is difficult, but it is nevertheless a most necessary task which should be done, wherever possible, with the knowledge and cooperation of the parents. In a few cases, parents were not being told all the reasons for visits, and this raises moral questions. No matter how sincere the motive – and in one instance, it was to maintain a relaxed environment on which to make an assessment of a child – it is not acceptable as professional practice. It also charges the arguments of those who associate home visiting with prying.

While many teachers recognized the potential of such contacts, they also stressed the importance of handling them with sensitivity. Even teachers who were strongly committed to home visiting were opposed to the idea of ever compelling a member of staff to go into homes, but they were in favour of providing the necessary training and support for those who wanted to. It was not always clear, however, how this support could be provided. There were obvious difficulties as far as timetabling was concerned if visits were made in the daytime. Even if they were made in the evening and time off in lieu was available, again this had implications for timetables and created problems which could not always be resolved. While one head-teacher said she would be willing to arrange cover if a teacher wanted to go into homes, without an established system this may be difficult both to request and organize. In many situations, home visiting is sustained by the goodwill of teachers who give up their free time without hope of recompense. In at least one case, the introduction of directed time had made a teacher reconsider this commitment and, whereas in the previous year she had visited in the evenings, this had come to an abrupt halt.

Many of the issues which emerge from this chapter stem from the way information is conveyed to parents. In Dalebridge Nursery School, for instance, parents were not sure why they had been asked to take their children to the pre-nursery groups, even though they attended regularly and were pleased to have the opportunity to do so. The teachers themselves presented different views on the aim of the groups, with the educational home visitor (EHV) seeing them as a preparation for school and the headteacher saying that this was definitely not the case. With concepts such as compensation and modelling underlying much of the work in the groups, the EHV may have been concerned neither to label the children nor to identify the groups too closely with 'problems'. Some people would question the value judgements which underpinned this arrangement, while others would want to ensure that those running such a group were highly trained and had appropriate skills. Potentially, it was a highly complex situation to negotiate. Simply because the situation is a difficult one, however, does not mean that the obligation to be explicit can be side-stepped.

The book and toy libraries were not used as much as they could have been, but it appeared that little encouragement or explanation about them had been given to parents. In one school in particular, the teachers overestimated the number of parents who used the book library and, although they described it as an excellent facility, the parents were less enthusiastic. Similarly, although the headteacher spoke of her desire to "educate parents" about appropriate toys, there was no evidence of how this was attempted other than to provide toys.

The findings in this study were similar to those of Tizard *et al.* (1981). Their research indicated that neither the parents of children from middle-class areas nor those from 'disadvantaged' areas were enthusiastic about this kind of library. The 'middle-class' group considered that their children already had 'developmental' toys and that the ones to be borrowed were too easy for them. The parents in the 'disadvantaged' areas had different criteria for judging toys and different expectations of them. They expected children to play without adult intervention and, in addition, they did not want to take responsibility for toys which belonged to the school. It is possible that, if teachers gave more explanation of toys and of play in general, and talked more about the books available, they would counter the feelings of many parents that these toys and books were not for them. Again, it is an extremely difficult role for teachers to adopt, for it has to be one that allows them to influence without appearing to patronize.

The video and the home visits in Stanfield Middle School raise other questions about effective communication with parents. There were problems in the way visits were arranged. Some related to a breakdown in communication between the home and the school, while others were connected to the fact that they were made only during the daytime, when some parents would not be available. Similarly, it is unfortunate that such a sizeable proportion of the parents interviewed seemed to have slipped through the net and did not see the video because of its rather haphazard method of distribution. Both the home visits and the video were seen by the school as key elements in their contact with parents and a great deal of importance was placed on them, yet they were not reaching all families. There was the danger that because the visits were school policy, and because it was assumed that the video reached more homes than it did, many parents were thought to have more information than in fact was the case.

In relation to the contents of the video, although one of the teachers commented on what she described as its "hidden ethos" which, she said, assumed its Asian audience were somehow "backward", no parent referred to a similar unease. Nevertheless, it is regrettable that, given the importance attached to its content by most of the teachers and given the audience which it was intended for, it was not produced in community languages. It did seem that the question of communication in general was underestimated by some teachers in the school, who did not see problems in their inability to speak to parents in their community language. Observation of some of the home visits did not substantiate this optimism and there were many instances where teacher and parents were not communicating to any significant degree.

All the parents who were involved with the Early Years Support Team were pleased to have had that contact. They reported specific skills which they had learnt, as well as ways in which they had been helped to change or adapt their attitudes. It was a service which brought parents and teachers into the kind of close contact which is experienced in few other settings, and the parents' response was very positive. Any criticism was reserved for other professionals, when they were seen to obstruct the benefits which could have resulted from the co-operation of the family and the team. The fact that the channels of communication with the team had been so open made it harder for them to accept 'surprise' assessments from others with whom they had had ongoing contact and the rapid judgements of those whom they did not know.

Some of the examples presented in this chapter indicate a cause for concern. It was clear that sometimes the messages which were being given to parents were at best confusing, and at worst misleading. For a variety of reasons, materials and services designed to increase parents' involvement with their children were not always explained to parents or made available to them. But despite these problems, there was still reason to have a cautious optimism for the future because it was clear that many parents and teachers want to improve and extend the contacts which they have with each other and are keen to develop strategies to facilitate this.

7 Day-to-Day Contacts between Home and School

Introduction

Much of the information collected in this research was about specific initiatives introduced into schools to facilitate contact between parents and staff. This chapter contains information about more routine, 'every-day' contacts, some of which are relevant to all schools and others which are widespread practices. Parents were asked about Parents' Associations and whether they felt that staff were responsive to their concerns. Parents and staff were asked about sessions to discuss children's progress, channels for routine contact and whether they had any suggestions for improvements to the way in which schools made contact with parents. There were also questions about written assessments, open records and several other forms of written communication. The responses to these general questions have implications for the development of any work with parents, as they are an indication of what parents and staff currently see as feasible and/or beneficial.

Parents' Associations

The main feature of the Parents' Associations discussed in this research was their role in fund-raising. Parents were generally positive about the Associations, although few had taken an active role and some were put off by their perception of the groups as 'cliques'. Non-participation was not indicative of a lack of interest in the school. An insight into just how 'exclusive' such groups could be was provided in Marksbury Comprehensive, where almost none of the parents interviewed had heard of the school's Home–School Association. One mother, who herself had been active in the Association for the past two years, threw light on why this was; she explained it thus:

> If I have one complaint about the school, this is it. We were asked in the second year to join. We had one letter sent home. Robert had been really worried because he'd been called to the head of year's office with a few other children but it had only been to get the original letter. I haven't got a clue why these children were chosen, but although the school's intake comes from about four schools, most of these parents were from the same primary school. We all went up and we hadn't a clue really why we were going. You have to remember that in the first year we had virtually no contact with the school because of the teachers' action. They explained that each year has a teacher who is supposed to gather his or her group of parents together and you talk about fund-raising, organizing events, gripes and complaints. Then all the groups should come together in a meeting and all the ideas and comments are thrown in.

It was sometimes difficult for parents to join in if they chose to. One mother from Lane End Infants School who attended ten meetings said that she was not really sure what she had contributed. She described the meetings as badly run and said that, "nobody really wants to hear anybody else's opinion".

There was general agreement from the staff that Associations were to be welcomed, although there was very little active involvement on their part. Banthorpe Comprehensive School's Parent–Teacher Association was unusual, in that it was active in both fund-raising and organizing evening events to discuss a variety of topics including technology and the problems of adolescence. It had run a course about governors which was attended by 90 people. Similarly, in Stanfield Middle School, the Association had recently begun to organize events based on religious festivals, which were attracting a much greater level of support from ethnic minority parents.

Open/consultation evenings

Sessions were held in all the schools visited for parents and staff to have one-to-one contact about individual children. The most common frequency was twice a year and the maximum number of meetings each year in any one school was three.

The parents saw limited value in these sessions but felt that it was important to go, and the majority of them had attended such meetings. In Tatehill First School (where most of the parents of new entrants had attended a meeting to discuss their child's progress and hear teachers explaining how maths and English were taught), the parents were enthusiastic in their response. "Essential", "fascinating", "crucial" and "reassuring" were words used to describe this meeting.

Parents in other schools and schemes selected for case-study work were more muted in their responses. In Lane End Infants School, the most common response from parents was that they felt they had a duty to go but that nothing new was learnt. Of the quarter who had not attended, one said that she knew how her children were progressing anyway, and another said that her limited understanding of English meant that there was no point in her going. There was nothing in the interviews to suggest that these parents were less 'interested' in their children than the parents who did attend. Practical problems, mentioned by both groups, included not enough notice being given of dates, problems of transport, difficulties of shift workers and lack of babysitters. One father was not alone in finding the sessions unduly time-consuming; he explained that his son:

> brings home a timetable, a list of times when you can see teachers. You tick the names of the teachers you wish to see and then it comes back with a time next to each name. But then when you get there and look around, you find some of the teachers haven't turned up or they have left their desks or there is an enormous queue in front of you. It is all a matter of negotiating your way around then and slotting in where you can.

The impression given by staff was of brief and rushed meetings with limited privacy, although they saw them as of value. The meetings were well attended; the lowest figure given for parental attendance was 70 per cent.

It was not always clear what the purpose of the sessions should have been. They were not a forum for discussing problems, as they were not held in private. In Stanfield Middle School, the first of three meetings held each year was designed not to discuss progress, but to give parents the opportunity to get to know staff and vice versa, and for parents to give information. In Tatehill First School, the aims were to "talk about children's good points as well as the areas where parents can help at home" and to "give a long-term perspective on children's work". The acting headteacher of Woodvale Comprehensive said that it was unrealistic to expect open evenings to serve a vital role in the information system, and he hoped that eventually they would disappear and be replaced by individual dialogue, as required, between parents and teachers. He felt that to invite parents into school to praise children at a standard time was not appropriate and that to wait for such a session to raise concerns or problems was unhelpful.

Routine contact with staff

There were clear differences between primary and secondary school parents' responses because informal daily contact was potentially available to the former group. Some parents took the opportunity to chat as they brought and collected their children, although it was more common to speak when there was a specific point to be made or a query to raise about their child. Parents laid great store by the contact they had with their child's class teacher. They valued a constructive response to their overtures and took a "no news is good news" view of the teacher's communication to them, trusting that they would be contacted as appropriate.

In the primary school in Planeborough, there was considerable variation in how often parents made contact with the class teacher, although all had attended at least one of the two consultation sessions available. However, it was still only one-third who contacted the class teacher at all (other than on consultation evenings), unless there was a problem to be solved.

One striking point to emerge from Lane End Infants School was the very positive views held of the headteacher, often based on limited contact, but which were sincerely held and expressed. Statements made by parents included "a committed person with good ideas", "the head is always around" and "makes herself available". Her concern when children were tired or unwell was clear to parents and was commended.

Staff in primary schools saw the periods of time before and after school as obvious occasions for dialogue. Staff were positive about this contact, describing it as "thoroughly enjoyable and useful for both sides" and seeing themselves as "approachable". All the headteachers in Planeborough stressed their accessibility. A typical response was: "Whenever possible, I see the parent immediately."

In the secondary schools, access to staff had to be negotiated by parents and little contact was reported, beyond organized sessions, by most members of staff. Although the acting headteacher in Overlea Comprehensive School, for example, had said that the procedure for parents to visit tutors outside consultation sessions was very straightforward and parents would be able to arrange a convenient appointment at home or at school, none of the tutors reported receiving any visits from parents. A small number of home visits had, however, taken place and some parents had telephoned tutors in school and, occasionally, at home.

In Marksbury Comprehensive School, parents contacted the year head if they wished to discuss anything, or even if their child was ill. There was very little opportunity for tutors to have any contact with parents other than on an arranged evening or if the year head involved the tutor directly. The deputy headteacher, the curriculum coordinator and five of the seven tutors would have liked to have modified this, so that more direct contact would be possible. It was acknowledged that the tutors knew the pupils well, given their contact over a number of years, and that it was inappropriate for sole authority to be invested in the year heads.

In Banthorpe Comprehensive School, the system was to contact either the headteacher or the head of House, with the former stating that he saw at least two or three parents each week. But the difference in approach by two heads of House was striking. One expected to see ten or so parents each half-term, with telephone calls from others; the other expected to have either personal or telephone contact with this number each week and was keen to develop a situation where parents' visits and calls were not just in relation to "negative happenings".

The responsiveness of staff to parents' concerns

In more than one-half of the schools where the question of staff responsiveness to the concerns of parents was asked, virtually all the parents said that they felt that teachers would tackle any issues that parents raised with them.

In three of the schools, however, a sizeable minority of parents did not feel that teachers were responsive. In Marksbury Comprehensive School, specific incidents were recalled, relating to option choices, disciplinary matters and a situation where children had apparently been "abandoned" by the teacher during a school trip. On the last point, one father said that his contact with the headteacher over this incident had made him think that "They give you the feeling that they will be responsive and yet they aren't. I spoke to the head about it, he nodded and seemed to agree but he didn't report back to the parents, so it was an impression of being responsive rather than a reality." In Overlea Comprehensive School, parents said that teachers varied in their attitude to parents' queries. One referred to a science teacher who had responded to her concerns about her daughter's progress by laughing and saying that her daughter was "not stupid". The feeling of frustration was encapsulated by the father who said that:

> They just give you the bit of information they want to give you to get the answer they want. At the GCSE options meeting there was a lot of concern that they are doing mixed science and that this would not be acceptable as an A-level base. The acting head was standing there saying they had been in touch with all the colleges and they would accept it, but we've only got his word for that... Parents' concerns about this were passed over, but these sort of things are very important.

Improving contact

There was variation in the number of parents in each school who would have liked to see changes in the contact available to them. There was only one school (in Planeborough) where a majority of those interviewed had suggestions. Two of these parents wanted more constructive ("no flannel") open evenings. But a substantial proportion said that they would have liked to have fewer parents helping in school. This point was summarized by the parent who said: "It sometimes seems as if there are more parents than teachers...it's all too much and they stand back in judgement and make their opinions known about other people's children and I think it's all wrong really." Others felt uncomfortable about parents 'teaching', as with the parent who said: "There's instances where other parents are teaching our children with no teaching qualifications. I totally disagree with it. It should be discouraged, but it's encouraged and the teachers seem to think that they might gain something out of it."

In the other settings, it was between one-third and one-fifth of parents who gave suggestions for changes they would like to see. Most of the comments were about the inefficient organization of consultation sessions to discuss progress. There were requests for open evenings to be more frequent and less rushed with more flexible appointment times, that is day and evening. Some parents suggested allocating certain days after school for staff to discuss individual children with their parents, in addition to the present "formal" meetings.

Staff said that they would like to be continually developing their work with parents; for example: "The school has worked very hard for changing and improving; always doing it, always ongoing." Very few specified possible improvements. Some suggestions were that there should have been more extensive informal contact with parents, that parents should have been more involved in transition and that they should have received more information about what was done in school.

Written assessments

One method of communicating with parents about individual children is by preparing a written assessment of progress. Both the parents who were currently in receipt of written assessments, and those who were not, clearly saw them as of value.

The parents of secondary-aged pupils received written accounts of their children's progress and were, on the whole, happy with them. In Marksbury Comprehensive School, for example, the vast majority of parents said they had received two reports since their children started school, that is two reports in three years. They had not received any reports during their children's first two years in school because of the teachers' industrial action. This was the least frequent reporting in the secondary schools studied, and while one-half of the parents were satisfied with the number of reports, the others would have liked them to appear more frequently, so that parents were alerted to problems at an early stage. As one parent commented: "His last report suggested that he had been messing around since September – had we known earlier we would have leant on him but we would have liked to know earlier... There were 14 entries on his behaviour, so it must have been fairly general."

The most detailed response to this question came from the group of parents in Overlea Comprehensive School whose children were experiencing difficulty with reading. They were very keen to have written comments which gave an idea of the rate at which their child was making progress and of what had been achieved, as well as reassurance that any difficulties were being recognized and dealt with. A great deal of dissatisfaction was expressed about the paucity of information from the primary schools their children had attended. One mother said that she had only become aware that her son was experiencing problems when he told her that someone was coming into school to do extra work with him. She had only discussed her son at open evenings and had not been approached by staff directly. She was critical of the open evenings because there was no privacy and she was embarrassed at hearing negative comments about her son in front of other parents. One couple recalled not being told that there was any problem until their son was nine or ten and the mother explained that she had thought everything was "hunky-dory" and that he "just wasn't interested in doing things at home". Coupled with the fact that several of them had been concerned about their child's development from an early age, this had resulted in very anxious times for the parents concerned.

In Stanfield Middle School, written assessments had been introduced in response to parental requests and all parents said that they welcomed these, and most would have liked to receive them twice a year.

In the schools for younger children, written assessments were not available, although a sizeable number of parents would have liked them. They wanted a general account of how their child was progressing with details of strengths and weaknesses. Concerns were expressed that oral exchanges were easily forgotten and teachers may have focused on personality rather than attainment. The vagueness of some statements, for example, "Oh, he's fine", was criticized. Parents felt that they did not have enough information "to understand progress".

There was some variation in the teachers' views on written assessments, at least in the primary sector. The concern was that inappropriate measures would be used that could have a detrimental effect on the pupils. In Stanfield Middle School, all staff were in favour of written reports as long as they gave a rounded assessment of the child and did not contain categories that suggested "pass" or "fail". In Lane End Infants School, staff were divided, with one-half of them feeling that an oral assessment was sufficient for a child of this age. Those who would have welcomed written accounts stressed the need to focus "on the whole child and not just learning". It was said that these should not include class position or any grading.

Open records

Another issue in assessment is whether records on individual pupils should be open to their parents. This was policy in two of the LEAs where case-study work was undertaken. The overwhelming majority of parents in all schools said that records on individual children should be open to their parents. Typical comments were: "It's nice to actually know you can look at things like that if you really want to" and "It's your child. And I don't see why they should be secretive." The few reservations expressed were that teachers would be reluctant to record certain things if parents had access, for example, suspected child abuse, and that such documents would inevitably be "bland".

In one school where records were open to parents, two-thirds of them were unaware of this fact; and in the other, it was just over one-third. In this latter school, most could recall being told about the records when their child started school. Only one had asked to see them and she had been surprised by the form this took. She had approached the school secretary and been told that she needed to make an appointment with the headteacher to look through the file. The session had gone very well but she had been rather taken aback by the formality, as this was not the impression she had been given when she had first heard about the records from the headteacher.

The overwhelming majority of staff were in favour of open records. There was only one teacher in one school, and two in another, who expressed disagreement. Otherwise it was felt that "It's part of life that things should be more open" and "It has to be the way to work". One teacher said that it would encourage staff to take more care with the wording of what was written, explaining that "perhaps teachers got away with too much like this in the past".

There was a general feeling that a professional approach would ensure that the system worked; for example: "If you have a child who has caused trouble or concern in some way, you should be able to write that in a professionally appropriate way that would be reasonable for parents to see." What was not resolved from their responses was how to deal with sensitive information of a broader kind, perhaps referring to aspects of children's home life which were of concern.

Written communication

Parents were asked for their comments on the written communication they received from school. This included newsletters, letters, the Governors' Report and the school handbook. The parents were generally appreciative of the information sent to them, although much of it was routine and their comments were low key. The majority of parents in most schools said that they would have liked more information about the school and the curriculum.

A few references to the unreliablity of pupils taking correspondence home were made across the schools, schemes and services selected for case-study work. Parents also spoke of receiving what seemed to be an excessive number of letters. In Lane End Infants School, regular newsletters were produced, and it was striking that all but one of the parents said they had read them and the majority of parents were extremely positive about their content and regularity. Some correspondence was not written in an accessible style, and little written information on matters other than routine was distributed. The difficulty of communicating by letter on more substantial topics was raised by the parent who said that the letter distributed about tertiary education would have been "heavy going", unless he had been involved in the discussions and heard all the arguments.

Curriculum statements

Curriculum statements were prepared in one comprehensive school to convey information to parents about what and how pupils were taught in each subject area. All the parents who were interviewed thought that these were potentially a valuable way of providing parents with information about the courses which their children were doing. All the staff were positive about these documents and saw benefits for pupils, parents and staff. The acting headteacher said that he felt that "parents have the right to information in an accessible manner". His aim was to "involve parents in the learning process and in the planning process", and he saw these documents "as the starting-point".

The statements sent to parents contained some complex sentences. It was unclear, for example, what was meant by the course that "shows the pupils how the abstract and inexpressible religious truths may be depicted in dance, drama and the fine arts". A parent unfamiliar with the subject-matter or vocabulary of that description would gain precious little insight into what their child was doing. Similarly, to read that "The English course is structured around skills and processes, not content" may add little to the parents' understanding of what was taught.

There was a lot of support for curriculum statements in principle, and a feeling that such documents were worthwhile in practice. One teacher, who was herself a parent, described an incident when she had been able to liaise successfully with her son's teacher in relation to maths, and said that parents who "don't know the system" in this way really were at a disadvantage.

Discussion

A variety of day-to-day contacts have been discussed in this chapter and some areas for potential development have been identified. Parents' Associations could potentially enhance the exchange of information and quality of relationships between home and school; however, there was little evidence of this from the ones studied in this research. There were indications of wider roles for Associations in schools that go beyond fund-raising but considerable efforts would be required to establish and develop them. Whatever aims Associations have, it seems crucial that they strive to absorb newcomers and to value their contributions and do not reinforce the perception which some parents have of them as 'cliques'.

The limitations of some established forms of communication with parents were evident from the comments on open evenings and written communication. The value of open evenings was clear, but given the wide range of issues of both a general and confidential nature that could be covered in these sessions, it is vital that they form only one strand of a much wider system of contact between home and school.

For many parents, sessions to discuss their children's progress (as presently organized) were attended as a matter of course, rather than because a great deal was gained from them. Parents appreciated learning about the curriculum and welcomed concrete, clear information about how their children were progressing. Again, however, there were practical considerations which meant that some parents could not attend – a fact that was not always appreciated by teachers.

Sessions in all but one school were held in the evenings. Overlea Comprehensive had established daytime sessions during the period of teachers' industrial action, and they were now seen by staff (although not always by parents) as the most productive arrangement. Staff were critical of parents who were not prepared to come, although they would have to rearrange working commitments to do so, and of fathers who were "too grand and too busy to come".

There was very limited routine contact with staff for most parents and this was, largely, rather superficial. Contact was 'problem-focused' and there was little evidence of ongoing contact about children's development and learning. Parents were positive about their access to staff when they really needed it, but there was still a feeling of needing a reason to make contact. Flexible 'open' lines of informal communication would be required if parents and staff were to exchange information and ideas on a wider range of issues.

Although there was a general belief in the responsiveness of staff, it was clear that there was potential for significant conflict when disagreements or breakdowns in communication occurred. There were situations where parents had been dissatisfied with how their concerns had been dealt with. Their comments highlighted some of the demands made on teachers when complex issues are being discussed and the potential for dissatisfaction when parent and teacher have different views and expectations. One mother expressed the view that teachers tend to "shut-out" what they don't want to hear, and described her son's class teacher as a very "bubbly" person who "doesn't *really* listen".

Staff saw the development of their work with parents as a long-term process which should be continually developing. The parents' suggestions for change focused on more immediate concerns, in that they wanted more information about their children's progress and about what schools were providing.

When asked about the value of written assessments of pupils' progress, the parents were very positive, and this applied both to those who did, and those who did not, currently receive them. They wanted to know about academic progress and all-round development. Teachers were obviously concerned about the style and content of any such documents, and were wary of developing any system that would work to the detriment of primary school pupils by putting undue and unnecessary pressure on them.

There were indications (from the schools that provided them) of a tendency to rely on written reports to convey information about pupils which could usefully have been communicated earlier. Without even these formal and infrequent statements, information may simply not be communicated at all, as was described by the parents from Overlea Comprehensive School whose children had experienced difficulty in primary school.

The vast majority of parents and staff felt that children's records should be open to parents, and no insurmountable problems were envisaged in doing this, provided that they were written in an accessible style. What emerged clearly was the need for children to be discussed in an ongoing way, particularly when there were problems, rather than relying on official reporting times (whether these were oral or written). The information collected suggests that the approaches to assessment being introduced into schools, for example, profiling and records of achievement, will meet with general approval.

The potential benefits of curriculum statements in informing parents of their children's work were stated. It is vital that information is presented clearly and is detailed enough to be meaningful. Brief paragraphs will achieve little more than an opening for parents and staff to talk together. The descriptions of courses should avoid jargon and spell out in an intelligible way what will actually be done.

There were pointers from the comments made both by staff and parents to ways in which future developments should proceed. The references made by parents to more, and fuller, information about their children's progress and about their concern that there were too many parents in school are of particular interest. The second point concerns the need to clarify the purpose of different forms of contact between home and school and to communicate this intent to parents. It was also apparent that teachers were sometimes reticent about informing parents about negative aspects of children's behaviour or pro-gress and this would indicate the need for training in how to deal with such sensitive issues.

8 The Organization of Involvement

Introduction

This chapter is concerned with professionals who were appointed specifically to develop work with parents. It includes the work of three teams, two advisory teachers and an educational home visitor (EHV), whose remit involved working directly with parents or encouraging the development of such work.

The Planeborough Working with Parents Team comprised teachers on secondment who worked with their teaching colleagues to develop a range of initiatives in schools. The Stileborough team had a similar brief but undertook more work directly with parents, and staff were appointed to the team, rather than seconded. The third team (in Newborough) worked with young children with special educational needs and their parents in their homes.

The Millshire advisory teacher worked with several schools developing home–school reading initiatives, while in another authority an advisory headteacher provided support for several schools, including Overlea Comprehensive, which wanted to extend any aspect of their contact with parents. Finally, the work of the EHV based in Dalebridge nursery school is discussed.

The last section gives details of training to develop work with parents undertaken by teachers interviewed during this study, and their views on such training.

Planeborough Working with Parents Team

The type of work undertaken with schools

The team's aim was to provide support for staff who were developing work with parents in schools. As well as working alongside teachers in schools, they encouraged schools to develop a clear policy on work with parents and they said they acted as a "vehicle for promoting change", helping schools move "from involvement to partnership". The team developed specific initiatives in schools, responded to one-off requests for advice and maintained contact with schools which were no longer receiving regular support.

One of the tasks was to help schools work with the parents of pre-school children. And one headteacher had been rather concerned about the number of children whom he defined as 'disadvantaged' coming into the reception class and the many children who were 'not ready' for nursery. In this school, there were discussions between staff and a team member, who was seen as someone with whom they could "kick ideas around" and talk through the various ways in which they could work. As a result, four half-day workshops for parents were established and six booklets, also for parents, on different topics were produced. Each booklet was designed to show activities which parents could do with their children at home to support what was done in the nursery. The workshops were intended to enable parents to understand more about the process of learning. The headteacher was very pleased with the workshops but unsure of how much change they had promoted or could be expected to promote. They certainly did not result in parents having the continuing contact that the school would have liked, as they were discontinued when support from the team ceased because staff time was not available.

In another school, which only offered children one year in the nursery, there was pressure from parents who felt that their children needed more than a mother and toddler group. Two members of the team were involved in establishing a pre-nursery group. They worked with the headteacher for six months and, when they withdrew, the group continued albeit with some difficulties. When it had started in the February, eight parents brought their children; by the September it had grown to 14. It had been allowed to expand because the school expected that students from the child care course in the local community secondary school were going to help. This did not happen and the headteacher struggled to run it herself with occasional help from a nursery nurse student. In the long term, various offers of help were made, but the headteacher was conscious of having felt an enormous commitment to making the idea survive after the team's withdrawal.

One reception class teacher had used a team member to cover her class, so that she could make home visits to groups of four or five mothers meeting in one house. She took games with her and loaned them to parents to play with their children. The team's support had acted as a focus, given the work impetus and, on a practical level, provided the cover. When it came to an end, the school secured a supply teacher, funded from the authority, and so the visits have continued.

Another major area of work for the team was its involvement in an infant school, where the headteacher had wanted to move away from highly formal learning activities in the nursery, and to do this with the support of the parents. Following discussion with the team about the school's philosophy in general and its approach to parents, a meeting for parents was held. The proposed changes were discussed and parents of nursery children were invited to six daytime workshops on what happens in a reception class. It was hoped to "win parents over by showing them successful practice", and the demand from parents to attend was such that three groups were planned. At each one, language activities, practical maths and creative activities were explained and a member of the team worked with children alongside the teachers. At the end of the first six weeks, parents were asked to evaluate the sessions. Although very few evaluation sheets were returned, those parents who did reply suggested that the course had been presented in a patronizing way, and that parents felt uneasy about observing and unsure whether they should join in.

These comments were taken into consideration in planning the next course. The sessions were shorter, and there was an introduction to the themes that were being followed through in the nursery, to give parents a foundation from which to use the classroom experience. In addition, the team extended their original brief by working with those teachers in the school who were not completely happy about the proposals because they felt that this work with parents had been imposed on them.

Another infant school wanted to involve parents in curriculum development. The headteacher was concerned because this was not carried through in the policies of the junior school on the same site, and sought the assistance of the team to develop an Infant and Junior links programme. Having identified one teacher in the junior school who wanted to participate, plans were being made to identify a way forward. The headteacher knew and trusted the experience of the team member involved, so was confident that she would not "do too much too quickly or bulldoze the staff and so destroy what we were aiming at".

The team's perspective

The team was staffed entirely by teachers on secondment, working one day a week on the team, in most cases for a year. While an element of continuity was provided by two members who had been with the team since it began, concern was expressed in all the interviews about a staffing arrangement that was dependent on secondments.

The inspector responsible for the team felt that, at a time of competing priorities, work with parents would be neglected. With so little time available and so much being attempted in schools and in-service sessions, there was little opportunity for discussion and review:

> I've seen them meeting at eight in the morning, and at six at night, catching up. It is an unfair onus...the commitment of the staff is wonderful but it is all very uncertain, especially at the moment. We try to plan for the next 12 months but we can only get the go-ahead for a term in advance.

Although the headteacher, who was seconded to the team, regarded it as an opportunity for teachers to widen their viewpoint, she saw the fact that they had to pick up the work for just one day a week as a real problem. She had a degree of flexibility not available to class teachers, so if she needed to see someone at a time other than on the allotted day, she could fit it in. While her colleagues on the team were generally positive about their involvement, there were references to the difficulties of adjustment to this work for a one-year period and for just one day a week.

This must have been all the more difficult because not all secondees had a particular expertise in this area of work. One teacher said she had found it very hard to understand all the different ways in which parents could be involved:

> There is no definite format and there are so many different individuals and so many needs. I'm just getting used to it, and people are just getting used to me. It's a very sensitive area. Some staff don't want to do it. If it's done quickly, it's superficial. It takes two terms to build up your contacts, then it's time to go. So there's a whole wealth of information you just take away with you, that will just be disregarded.

Another teacher found she had insufficient time to do the job properly, but appreciated the chance to experience a variety of schools and curriculum areas. She had not heard of the term "partnership with parents" before coming on to the team. Working on the team had opened her eyes to initiatives, but she was still unclear about how decisions were made, how it was decided what each member would do and whether a long-term plan existed.

Headteachers' views on the work of the team

The headteachers of the schools that had received this support welcomed the team's involvement and appreciated the support. It had helped teachers to clarify their ideas and the practical help had enabled ideas to be implemented. One newly appointed headteacher said that she considered the team to be the best way for her school to initiate work with parents because the school had to overcome both a long history of non-involvement of parents and staff reluctance:

> I needed someone reliable to make the contacts and follow them through. We needed to take small steps because of the history of the school. In the past, parents have not been encouraged to come into the school. The odd teacher would have had a parent in to help but that would be it. So you can't jump from that to full parental involvement.

Another headteacher mentioned how much he had benefited from being able to talk about ideas when he was "fresh, and not jaded at the end of a day or when I am dashing around at dinner time".

Those initiatives where there had been negotiations with teachers before the team worked alongside them were the most successful in meeting the team's objectives of achieving change. This did not necessarily mean that the original scheme remained intact. In some cases, having worked with parents in a particular way, the teachers adapted the scheme according to need and resources. There were instances where the team members worked with parents without the involvement of teachers from the school, but these initiatives were short-lived and did not carry on when the team's support ended.

Despite the many positive comments about specific instances, the majority of these headteachers also identified drawbacks to this form of provision. One was full of praise for the way the team member had worked with staff and parents, but still did not think that it was the right kind of support because it made parental involvement seem a separate issue rather than a fundamental part of school life. Another headteacher viewed it as a cheap way of getting things done and, in the long term, not a very satisfactory one. He stressed that although support from the team was "nice", it was no alternative to proper resourcing in schools, including adequate professional cover. The team was described as "throwing some sort of life-line" which had allowed the workshops and home visits to develop. The disadvantage of having to terminate involvement was a theme which underlay much of what the headteachers said. Concern was expressed about the danger of raising parental expectations and then failing to sustain the initiative. One headteacher's comment typified these views:

> these schemes need continuity and if you swop and change people around the parents lose faith. Particularly parents in this sort of area, they need one person to relate to and that person has to be the kind of person who can offer a bit of sympathy. The success of any projects depends on the nature of the people involved. This scheme works on a secondment basis, which produces no continuity. Projects need the same person to stay with them.

The first choice for most headteachers would have been more generous staffing allowances. An alternative arrangement would have been a team comprising permanent members who would have maintained contact until an initiative was firmly established.

Authority-level INSET provided by the team

A series of six INSET sessions was organized by the team for teachers in the authority. This consisted of five afternoons on different themes and an all-day conference. The conference gave individuals the opportunity to disseminate details of the various projects they were involved in to an audience of parents and teachers. Many teachers said they were aware of developments 'out there' but were unsure about how to proceed in their own circumstances, and the sessions were designed to meet this need.

The five sessions covered: why schools should want to work with parents, parental involvement in reading, communication with parents, the establishment of courses for parents and the development of a whole-school philosophy towards a partnership with parents. Teachers who had received support from the team described their work, and there were some group sessions using a Working with Parents training pack (De'Ath and Pugh, 1986).

There were also opportunities for teachers to relate their own experiences of work with parents. Occasionally the session leaders attempted to make those present reflect on their own practice, but these comments did not seem to stimulate thought or cause teachers to reconsider what they were doing. Many assumptions were allowed to go unquestioned. In one plenary session, for example, it was clear that a group of teachers looked on parental involvement mainly in terms of the problems parents brought to a situation and no attempt was made to question this perspective.

One teacher, who had been seconded to the team in a previous year, gave a talk on how she had started to involve parents in reading in the school where she worked. In the course of this, she said that a child's failure to read was caused by "uninterested parents" and parents who were "poor readers" themselves. She also explained her criteria for selecting parents in the initial stages of a project, having chosen them because "they brought their children to school themselves and took them home themselves. The children were reasonably well dressed and the parents obviously cared for them." If someone so closely associated with the team perpetuated these notions, without questioning them or being questioned, there must be some doubt about the value of the sessions in encouraging any development. The strong impression was that teachers had come to the course with a certain view of parental involvement and left with their commitment strengthened or their prejudices re-inforced.

School-based INSET provided by the team

One infant school invited parents to meetings to explain and discuss the school's reading policy. Two members of the team ran two after-school sessions for staff to prepare for these meetings. Much of the first session was spent considering what parents would want to know and what the teachers would want parents to know. The second session discussed a school booklet on reading, role plays and the organization of the meetings.

The teachers who attended found the sessions valuable and felt more confident about the planned meetings. The team was also involved in the organization and running of a six-session course for parents. The combination of the course and the training for her staff was just the type of support the headteacher wanted. She described this help as having been given in a way which had been neither "dogmatic nor didactic" and which had enabled the staff to take over completely when the team stopped coming in. But again, observation of the sessions raised certain issues.

It was clear, for example, that some of the teachers had encountered what they described as 'aggressive' parents in the past, and there was some apprehension about coping with parents who questioned the school policy on reading. Strategies for coping with, and defusing aggression were suggested, but it was apparent that not all the teachers felt comfortable with the school policy on reading. What seemed to underpin the proceedings was a desire on the part of the headteacher to convince parents about the way the school approached reading rather than to place parents firmly within that approach.

Various assumptions were challenged by the team members leading the sessions, but there was no suggestion that the school policy on reading should be fully explained to parents. While parents would be told, for instance, of the importance of regularly listening to their children read without the television on, and why children would sometimes bring books home that they could already read, there was to be no serious attempt to move beyond this. This assumption seemed to be that parents would not understand, or would disagree with, what the school was trying to do.

Parental Involvement in Education Team in Stileborough

Team members' views on their role

The team held the firm belief that parents and teachers should have a good understanding of one another. Members regarded themselves as "catalysts" and "enablers". They had regular review meetings to analyse their aims and progress and plan their development. An example of this was the way the nursery nurse's role had evolved from a part-time appointment as a crèche-provider to an independent participant in a wide variety of activities.

The team members referred to the difficulties involved in working in school, given their remit. They were in the schools but not "of them", and they sometimes said things that schools did not want to hear. One said how powerless she felt in some situations because, despite the enormity of the task, she was only in any school for a short period or for a single session. Ideally, she would have liked to have been responsible for a group of schools in which she could work intensively with an agreed contract and defined aims. She felt that because the team was so small and the number of potential schools to be worked with so great, the team was often forced to react to situations rather than plan their future involvement.

The members of the team all expressed a very strong attachment to their team identity. There were comments about the advantages of being able to call on one another's experience and expertise, and there were many instances where they worked together in homes and schools. The fact that there were other colleagues to provide support and stability was highly valued. They spoke of their need to come back to the office to 'let off steam' or talk a problem through, and referred to advisory teachers in other subject areas who had very isolated jobs.

Working with teachers and parents

The team worked in many different ways, in response to the needs of particular schools. This included running parents' groups and workshops, supporting parents in classrooms, working with parents and children in the home, and presenting talks on various topics at parents' evenings.

The team members expressed concern that school staff were not always informed of their proposed work:

> You can only presume that teachers have been consulted, even if you make it clear at the start that it is vital. This term I have been into two schools where the headteachers were newly appointed. They both believed in the importance of involving parents but it seemed to be completely new to the rest of the staff. They were antagonistic, which is perhaps not surprising given the situation. I could talk to them, but at the end I had to say "they are the issues, get back to me when you have decided what to do".

One of the principles which the team members adopted consistently was to make it clear to schools that they would do everything to support teachers who wished to work with parents; but if an individual was not comfortable with the work, it would not continue.

Some schools interpreted support as the provision of a substitute teacher to cover a class for a time. Although in some instances the team was willing to cover for a teacher who wanted to work with a specific group of parents or make home visits, they tried to discourage schools from regarding them in this light because: "It is a very expensive use of an allowance teacher. What I say to headteachers is that cover should be sorted as an internal management issue if the whole staff are co-operating; it is when ill-feeling starts that problems begin."

The team members made home visits and, in some cases, accompanied teachers. The head of the service saw this as one element of their in-service work with teachers who were reluctant or who lacked the confidence to go out on their own, and this type of support underpinned much of their work in schools. Occasionally a member of the team would run a group alone, but ideally the class teacher was expected to take part, even if only as an observer:

> if we go in and do it for them, it becomes the parental involvement Tuesday morning. And that is not what we want to see. We are there as advisory teachers and when we go into schools we should be concerned to raise awareness and examine the attitudes of the staff to parental involvement.

Attitudes encountered in school

The team members could all identify work which they thought had been successful or where schools had seized the initiative and gone on to work with parents. While they were all critical of some teachers' attitudes and of some headteachers' reluctance, there were positive comments about the shifts in attitudes and practice which could be achieved. There was a reference to one headteacher who had been very apprehensive about introducing a particular type of open evening where team members had spoken to parents. The reality was that parents had been very appreciative and there had been none of the aggressive questioning that had been feared.

In general, however, they still felt that there was a long way to go, particularly in encouraging schools to change their established practice. As one team member put it:

> When I took this job I did envisage some problems with motivating parents. I did not evisage any problems motivating teachers...teachers had had very positive attitudes to parents where I had taught. I thought it was the same in all schools. I think I can say, hand on heart, that I have had virtually no problems motivating parents, but I have had a number of heart-rending problems with teachers... Many stem from what I see as my responsibility to steer teachers away from the stereotype of what is a 'good family'.

The future of the team

The adviser was concerned about limited promotion prospects for the members of the team. While she wanted experienced, skilled staff, it often seemed like a 'dead end' once they worked outside schools. There was also a problem of funding. The original grant had been awarded for three years and after that the team was absorbed into the mainstream budget – and there was a threat that the team's budget would be withdrawn. The team members had permanent contracts with the authority and would be redeployed if the threat became a reality; but the lack of security was keenly felt by the adviser:

> Even if we survive, we may well lose this expertise. We are under threat at a time when every piece of research is indicating the importance of parental involvement. Our ultimate aim is to involve parents in their children's learning and that is their right. Some schools will achieve it and others will only touch on it. We have advanced a lot but now we are under threat. If this is how the LEA is going to prioritize parental involvement, I'd rather they hadn't bothered at all. I have a team of teachers working all out, and I am bitter that these teachers are now having to live with this threat.

Newborough Early Years Support Team

The team members' work

Each member of the team was extremely positive about her job. They all voiced appreciation of the satisfaction that comes from working with different families each day on an individual basis:

> It must be one of the most stimulating teaching jobs. It is intellectually stimulating in the way any teaching is because you are dealing with children, looking for progress. The degree of report-writing, and the like, is infinitely greater than that expected from any classroom teacher. The level of discussion about children is of a high level and just as a regular thing you'll be dealing with social workers, health visitors, headteachers, class teachers and doctors. And you deal with these people *yourself*.

They commented on the close working relationships which they had with parents and teachers, and on how the members of both these groups looked to them for advice and information.

The head of the service, who was very conscious of the potential for isolation within the job, emphasized how important it was for each of them to give the others support. Much of the week was spent working on their own, and meetings were valued as an opportunity to discuss individual cases and team plans, as well as a way of giving mutual support.

There were other pressures on the team because of the nature of their work. If a teacher was ill, for instance, nobody could make the visits. On a day-to-day basis, contacting fellow professionals to give or receive advice and the physical effort of travelling from family to family could be draining. Nevertheless, all members of the team clearly valued what they were doing very highly. They referred to the degree of commitment which was required of them and, despite working individually, the strength which they derived from working as a team. One teacher put this most clearly:

> In every decision we take, we refer back to our underlying philosophy, to question what the Education Act of 1981 was all about and ask how we could best apply the principles of Warnock. It has developed in this light, which I think makes it quite special. I am ever so proud to have worked on the team.

Team members' views on their work for parents

One of the main advantages for parents was seen to be the emotional support which such a service could give. There was a general recognition that parents had often heard only negative comments about their children from the professionals they had met. One mother had told a member of the team that she was "the only person who ever says anything nice about my child". Most of the parents had been told, at some point, that they had reason to be concerned about their children's development and the team appreciated how much anxiety this produced.

A number of potential problems were, however, recognized. For example, one member of the team suggested that she and her colleagues were so positive that parents were not always prepared for the disappointments which they sometimes had to face. In raising parents' expectations and encouraging them to aspire to their children going to mainstream schools, she hoped that they did not sometimes lead parents to have unrealistic goals for their children.

The team members saw themselves as being there to boost children's skills, whether there was a short- or long-term developmental delay or a problem which would require special educational provision at a later date. But these skills had to be transferable to school because it was there that decisions about the children were made, and this was beyond the team's control. Similarly, because they worked with children on a one-to-one basis, teachers needed to be very conscious of the effect that this could have:

> from the brightest to the not-so-bright, given one-to-one attention, any child might do wonderful things. But the outside world isn't like that. It is about learning within a group, being able to adapt to distractions, group instructions, all that goes with group learning. If you so clue your child into an individual approach, you have disadvantaged the child and you will have disadvantaged him seriously.

It was not always easy for parents to recognize that. Because they had seen the progress that could be achieved, it was sometimes difficult to explain that more individual attention was not necessarily a "good idea".

The Millshire advisory teacher

The primary adviser, who had overall responsibility for the implementation of the home–school reading initiative, believed in a non-directive approach. This presented teachers with options which they could develop in their own way supported by the advisory teacher, who provided ideas, cover and practical help. In addition, the adviser saw her colleague as a sort of 'watchdog' who suggested which schools needed support and monitored their progress. She was conscious of the demands made on the teachers to prepare and check materials and link cards, and regarded the help given by the advisory teacher as a recognition of these demands.

The views of the staff in the schools

All but one of the schools had received some support from the advisory teacher at the beginning of their involvement in the scheme. The overall impression was that this help was valuable but that more centralized support would have been welcomed. This view was typified by the teacher who felt that the contact had been "very supportive; I would have been totally lost at the beginning without her help. It was just a mountain of materials and she was very helpful. I would have liked her to come in more to the sessions, but she could only come to the first one." Talking to someone who had contact with the other schools embarking on similar work was said by the same teacher to allow for "nice cross-fertilization".

Another teacher, who had spent a long time in the initial period preparing materials, would also have liked more of the advisory teacher's time, as well as a more directive approach from the authority. She said she had "got a bit cross about that at first because I thought of all the schools across the county doing much the same thing. I felt our time was precious and there could have been short cuts."

Two of the schools had been involved in the support group meetings and, although these groups were only in their early stages of development, the teachers who had participated thought that such contact with other teachers engaged in similar work would be of value. In one school, however, the teachers had decided not to attend because they felt that they would be contributing, rather than learning, and they did not wish to take on this extra demand.

In two schools, headteachers alluded to unease not articulated by the teachers themselves. This related to the proper replacement of staff while the teachers were working with children and parents. In one school, the headteacher was concerned that the only way to cover the rest of the class was to use the teacher with responsibility for special educational needs, and therefore her contact with children with learning difficulties was reduced. In the other instance, the headteacher acted as the replacement teacher, and she was very conscious of having to leave other demands to do this. That was threatening the future of the workshops in the school and there was some talk of abandoning them in favour of extending an existing lending scheme. Parents would still have access to the games and other materials, but would not be able to use them with their children in school.

It was difficult for the authority to have a clear idea of what the scheme provided because it was understood that the schools would develop it to suit their own needs. In addition, it was apparent that neither the adviser nor the advisory teacher thought that a thorough evaluation was appropriate. It did seem that there was a belief that it was based on a worthy premise and must therefore be extended.

The advisory headteacher attached to Overlea Comprehensive School: INSET

The advisory headteacher's main contribution to the school during her attachment was in the area of training. She was involved in a daytime session and a series of after-school meetings about home visiting.

The advisory headteacher's views

Although the advisory headteacher was conscious of some resistance from teachers to the ideas which she introduced, she thought that the daytime session had gone well. She was not so enthusiastic about her subsequent contact with the school. The first after-school session had consisted of a brainstorming exercise about the advantages of home visiting, followed by group discussions. The next two sessions, which the advisory headteacher was not able to attend, had been led by the first-year tutor (who had a strong commitment to home visiting) with the support of the head of the first year.

Twelve teachers had attended the first of these sessions, which were all in undirected time after school, and nine and six teachers respectively attended the second and third. Potential and actual home visits were discussed. At the end of the third week, it was agreed that when the advisory headteacher returned for the fourth meeting they should concentrate on how teachers could best deal with "difficult parents". They thought they would possibly use role-play techniques to act out different situations which they could find themselves in.

Yet it was only when the advisory headteacher arrived at the school for this session that she was told what they wanted to discuss. It had not gone well. As far as the advisory headteacher was concerned, it had not been well structured and the ten teachers who were there did not attend the session from start to finish, which was distracting. They had been told by senior staff to "pop along for the bits you can manage", but she had only subsequently learnt of this. The advisory headteacher had attempted to overcome that by asking those who wished to attend the sessions planned for the spring to give a time commitment and to submit ideas for how that time should be used. Early in the spring term she met with the first-year tutor and the year head to plan these sessions. In the event, only one other teacher attended the first of these and the one planned for the following week was cancelled.

When the advisory headteacher reflected on the experience, she expressed a great deal of disappointment about the lost opportunity for the school to make a firm commitment to home visiting. She was conscious of some early resistance both towards her and to one tutor whom she described as "so enthusiastic that she can be seen as very pushy and it may antagonize colleagues and make them defensive". Her main criticism, however, was reserved for school management. She saw the senior teachers in the school as apparently willing to take up the additional support given for work with parents without giving their real support to teachers to undertake the work. When the final training session was abandoned, she discussed with the head of the first year how she could continue to support this work in the school and they had decided that it should be the senior management team and senior tutors who should discuss the appropriate way forward. She heard nothing further from the school and it effectively marked the end of her contact with the school for that year.

The teachers' views

The overwhelming reaction from most of those interviewed was that the in-service sessions had generated considerable anxiety and stress among those who had attended. The participants did not have a clear understanding of what they should be doing in these meetings. One of the tutors, who said he enjoyed all his contacts with parents, had felt patronized by the approach, principally because he felt that a lot of assumptions had been made about him and what he was doing.

The acting headteacher certainly had some reservations about the role of the advisory headteacher conducting in-service training (INSET) when her background was not in secondary education. He had not attended the sessions but said he knew about the stress and pressure they had generated. He was aware that they had not been successful, but did not mention any discussions which had taken place in an attempt to improve future provision.

The school's evaluation of the support

Overlea Comprehensive School, like every other school that had received support from this LEA for work with parents, produced an evaluation of what had been achieved. This was written, in the first instance, by the teacher who had responsibility for home–school relations, and who was involved in the home-reading scheme. It was substantially re-drafted by a member of the senior management team before submission. The original report highlighted some of the problems which were encountered such as timetable constraints and the extra demands on already over-committed teachers. Mention was made of the attempts to encourage members of staff to use some of the 100 supply days to make home visits, which had proved unsuccessful. It was acknowledged that the assessment procedures in use for pupils made teachers reluctant to miss lessons; and that the timetable was such that sometimes teachers saw pupils only once every two weeks, and for this reason, it was not appropriate to miss any pupil contact time.

Lessons learnt

Everyone involved agreed that this work had not been productive, and it is possible to identify a number of reasons why this was so. While the interviews did not reveal why the advisory headteacher had felt she was subject to a degree of resistance and antagonism, some of the teachers were obviously unhappy with the content of the sessions, particularly with the role-play and other interactional games. It was not always clear to them what the advisory headteacher or the other group leaders were hoping to achieve. The planning and structure of the sessions needed more attention. There were also times when communication broke down and messages about what the advisory headteacher and the school expected of each other were not being passed on.

Beyond this, however, there was the serious problem of the apparent lack of commitment on the part of the senior management team. The school had requested the additional in-service support but this was not followed up by any attempt to show teachers that it was valued or to make it a priority in terms of time. There was no clear policy on home visiting and, without a strong commitment from the top, any training related to it was bound to remain a peripheral activity.

The educational home visitor in Dalebridge Nursery School

In contrast to working as a member of a team or as an advisory teacher in contact with a number of schools, the educational home visitor (EHV) on the Family Support Project in the nursery school worked on her own. She was employed for 12 hours each week, and most of this time was taken up with home visits and the pre-nursery groups. During the time the research team was involved with the nursery, the EHV moved to a full-time post in another school and a successor was appointed. This provided the opportunity to obtain two views on the same job.

Both women were very positive about the work of the EHV. They were committed to the idea of supporting families in this way and of drawing parents into the school at an early stage in the hope of establishing a long-term relationship. Both referred to the demands made by families where the parents and/or children had emotional problems, frequently compounded by economic or social hardship, but were positive about what they could potentially offer and about the stimulation which they received from the work. This is certainly reflected in what the former EHV wrote in one report:

> I have heard the post of educational home visitor described as 'a nice little job'. My description of it would be rather more glowing. I love my work. This is in no way meant to

diminish my awareness that it is physically demanding, can be emotionally exhausting and is very difficult to limit to a 12-hour week. The job carries with it considerable responsibilities and demands an acute awareness both of other people and oneself. The intention behind the job is the same as that found in all good educational practice – the all-round realization of the potential of each child.

The newly appointed EHV appreciated the opportunity to combine working with families with having a role in a school, although there were aspects which she found demanding, especially the fact of working so much on her own: "I am too much of a free agent: I would like more structure and more supervision. In a way, there's nothing I *have* to do. I've got to be quite strict with myself; I've no real statutory obligations."

The need to provide support for the EHV was clear. The member of staff who had left had certainly found the weekly supervision session with the headteacher helpful. Nevertheless, she believed that any further support would have to come from professionals who were already in contact with the families she worked with, such as health visitors and social workers, although she was unsure of how much professional status they would attach to the job of an EHV. This, of course, had implications for how much sharing of information there would be. There were no other similar posts in local schools, so there was no opportunity to draw support in that way or even to talk over individual perceptions of where the EHV's responsibilities ended.

In common with the advisory teacher teams, the EHVs pointed to the fact that there was no obvious career progression within the post. Both EHVs had sought out appropriate INSET sessions and had made contact with other services in the area. Because they were only employed for 12 hours a week, all the courses were in their own time, usually at weekends and in the evenings. They had identified the areas where they thought they needed support or development and had sought some appropriate solutions.

Training to work with parents

The difficulties encountered by the providers or consumers of the services described in this chapter have to be seen against the backcloth of national provision. Such additional resourcing is the exception, and for the majority of teachers the most likely form of support would be in the form of appropriate training. Atkin and Bastiani's research (1984) on training to work with parents has confirmed that 'much remained to be done in both initial training and in-service training', and it was therefore of interest to obtain the experiences of the teachers who were interviewed.

Initial training

Only three teachers said that working with parents had been covered in their initial training courses. One was a probationary teacher who had had a lot of contact with parents in the schools where she had carried out her teaching practice. Another remembered some discussion of the issue during initial training but this had not been reflected in the schools when he had been on teaching practice, where there had been "no real allusion made to contact with parents". The third could recall "something on parents in the Sociology of Education".

In-service training

Fifteen teachers had had relevant in-service training. This figure was artificially high because the research specifically focused on some situations where INSET had been organized. In some instances, for example, a particular initiative with parents was the subject of a case study of which training was one aspect. This was the situation in Overlea Comprehensive School, where six of the teachers interviewed had attended sessions on home visiting run by the advisory headteacher. The Newborough team worked on a one-to-one basis with parents and they had sought out appropriate training. The Stileborough teachers had attended sessions to extend their skills in working with parents. The remaining teacher, however, had done some in-service work about ten years previously.

About half the teachers questioned thought this type of training was necessary. In one school, for example, the headteacher and the other two senior teachers felt that young teachers needed to be aware of their responsibilities towards parents before their attitudes became hardened. One interviewee who did not see the need for INSET nevertheless thought it would be useful for experienced members of staff to talk about the importance of contact with parents with newly qualified teachers.

Some teachers held very clear views about the value of such training. Three distinct groups could be identified. There were teachers who wanted training in appropriate ways of working alongside parents, or involving parents in the life of the school. Others placed great store by the personality of the teacher and did not attach much value to training. The third group adopted a completely different perspective: they saw schools within a market-place, needing to 'sell' themselves. In such a situation, good public relations were essential and this required some training.

Discussion

Initiatives developed by staff going into schools may be a means of helping schools to examine their practices and develop their own policies. But there is a danger that such work will become compartmentalized and marginalized. The inspector in Plane-borough was very concerned about the consequences of this, especially as "parents' awareness will have been heightened and they will have different attitudes. It will all come unstuck if it doesn't go right through the school, if they go on to meet tea-chers without that philosophy."

It is also possible that responsibility for initiatives might be seen to reside with the external agency, rather than being transferred to the school. It is important therefore to negotiate and clarify at the outset the respective commitments of the external agency and the school. Examples drawn from the Planeborough Working with Parents Team well illustrated this point. In one school where the team's contribution had been carefully worked out in advance, the team members and the school staff had clear expectations of each other. The initiative survived both a first unsuccessful attempt to implement it and the team's departure. In another instance, where there was a last-minute decision to work in a school, the team member and one member of staff worked together in isolation from the rest of the staff. When they left, there was no way of recording or learning from the experience.

All this is, of course, related to the whole issue of staffing arrangements, and in some of the work which was examined the pitfalls of operating with secondees were highlighted. Two major difficulties were apparent: there is insufficient time for the seconded staff to develop initiatives with schools, and there are problems which arise from a lack of continuity. Although there are exceptions, both of these factors undermine two important requisites for success, as evidenced by the research. First, changes in attitudes of teachers and parents are more likely to take place where there is an atmosphere of trust fostered through mutual understanding. Secondly, success is more likely where the team works with teachers who are committed to the initiative and able to take control when the support is judged to be no longer needed.

Support work is, by its very nature, both demanding and complex. The staff go into school to fulfil many tasks. Not only are they expected to change attitudes and practice, but also to support and advise. The adviser in Stileborough decided to appoint staff at a higher point on the salary scale than was originally intended (even though this meant having fewer staff) because she wanted experienced people who would have "clout" in schools. It is, therefore, vital that they have significant experience and expertise upon which to draw. It is not justifiable to use secondment to this type of work solely as an opportunity to provide the *secondee* with new experiences.

It is also clear that professionals who are supporting the work need to be explicit about what they are able to offer. If this is not discussed, feelings of resentment may build up which may result in the kind of pessimism felt by the advisory headteacher working with Overlea Comprehensive School and the attendant negative attitudes generated in teachers. It is important for those who support work with parents to be clear about what they are able to offer in particular cases, and for the schools to be able to guarantee staff commitment. In return for giving their time and resources, the school and teachers are entitled to expect well-thought-out strategies.

Resources were not always used to their best advantage, most obviously where advisory teachers were used as substitute teachers. In Millshire, teachers in several schools made the same or very similar games, and while this meant that they became familiar with the materials, there was also a strong case for some central rationalization to avoid this duplication of effort. With regard to training, sometimes school-based provision is appropriate, but areas of work which are common to many schools may be better dealt with centrally. Where teachers want to understand more about how parents can be involved in reading with their own children, for example, there is a strong case for encouraging groups of schools to cooperate. There were many instances of small groups of teachers being told how to encourage parents and children to read together and how to produce the same type of booklet without any attempt at co-ordination or cooperation.

But even with good preparation and a clear idea of the objectives and methods, this type of work is very difficult. The views expressed by the Stileborough team indicate how much needs to be done. Even these teachers, who had a great deal of experience in the area, were faced with the reality of working with a large number of schools in which they were often able to do little more than react to problems as they arose. It was hardly surprising therefore that a teacher in Marksbury Comprehensive School had felt overwhelmed by the task that had faced him when he assumed responsibility for parental involvement. As a senior member of staff, he already had responsibility for implementing many new initiatives. Some years previously, a junior member of staff had been responsible for developing work with parents. The belief was that the post-holder had been unable to persuade colleagues to work with parents because she lacked seniority. Yet when a senior teacher was given the same time allocation of one half-day a week, he admitted that he was never able to use it for developing work with parents because of the many existing and competing demands on his time.

In some instances, the initiatives were being used to plug gaps in services. The most obvious area of concern was in the pre-school sector. While it is important to encourage parents to share a wider range of activities with their young children, and at times even to acknowledge that a project is compensating for a service which is not available, it should not be accepted as a permanent strategy for coping. Encouraging parents to bring their pre-school children into school to workshops or libraries is worthwhile, but it is not an alternative to the provision of nursery places. In all the pre-school initiatives studied in this research, additional resources, whether of staff, materials or other support, would have been valued. Work was being undertaken, in some cases, on very limited budgets and in an atmosphere of uncertainty about future security.

9 Key Issues and Some Implications for Practice

Introduction

This research has shown that developing work with parents can significantly improve what is provided by schools and services, but that the potential of this practice is frequently under-exploited. The superficial and problem-centred nature of much of the contact between parents and professionals meant that chances to capitalize on the opportunities for exchanging information and working together were lost. Such points are considered here and some of the principles behind, and goals of, work with parents are postulated. Some of the factors that characterize the most successful practice are presented, and the chapter ends with a consideration of how progress could be made.

The issues involved here are applicable to the whole age range. Managing transition was an issue for pre-school, primary and secondary schools. The need for detailed, clearly presented information about children's progress, what they are doing in school and for contact with staff was clear across all sectors. Parents' concern over their lack of knowledge about their children's school lives and, in some instances, the confusing and unhelpful contact they had experienced with staff were evident for all ages of children included in this study. This research has highlighted general principles for effective contact, for example, the need to ensure that goals are realistic. Thus, while staff will need to adapt the work they do with parents to suit their particular circumstances, the points raised by this study are of relevance to all those wishing to bring about improvements in their current practice.

Why involve parents?

Both parents and staff participating in this study pointed to considerable benefits that could accrue from systematic efforts to enhance the contact between parents and those with professional responsibility for their children. The parents who had received support in their homes for their pre-school children with special educational needs reported practical and emotional gains for themselves and for their children. The shared reading project for secondary school pupils who were experiencing difficulty showed how parents could be brought into their children's learning in a realistic and productive way. The teachers who had established workshops as part of the home–school reading initiative in primary schools were enthusiastic about their value for breaking down barriers with parents and enabling them to work together to achieve their shared goals.

The parents who had attended a course in an infant school to introduce them to how their children would be learning were able to identify insights and information they had gained. Spending time in classrooms had made it clear to parents that the classes were well organized and purposeful; it had helped them to understand their children's development and to participate in their learning in school. There is enormous potential for enhancing parents' involvement in this way, although the amount of time and planning required from staff to facilitate this must be acknowledged. An awareness of the provisions of the National Curriculum and of the attainment targets devised for the Education Reform Act 1988 will not, for example, automatically produce the level of awareness that was valued by some parents in this study.

Opportunities missed

Despite these clear benefits, there were numerous occasions on which chances for productive contact were missed or underused. The national surveys showed that there were serious discrepancies in the breadth, content and quality of service available to parents and in the support available to staff.

There were differences between, and indeed within schools, in what was expected of parents, which confused them and provided a 'hit-and-miss' element to satisfactory contact. There were situations where, for various reasons, neither parent nor staff would take the first step. These points may be illustrated by the evidence on children's reading development. Without a whole-school policy on how parents should be brought into this process, there was considerable variation in practice, and that annoyed and discouraged parents. It was clear that teachers' concern about putting undue pressure on parents by seeking their active involvement in their children's activities was not justified, and that parents felt frustrated when they were unsure about the best way to proceed with their children's education.

While there were meetings held for parents to explain the curriculum, or how something was being taught, these were frequently inadequately planned and failed to convey information in a clear and accessible form. There were situations where information or advice which would have been of more general interest was given only to those parents who had specifically asked for it. There were also occasions when advice was sought but the response had been unhelpful. Sometimes this was because it was not thought worthwhile for parents to be informed about their children's activities, and sometimes it reflected teachers' difficulty in describing their skills and practice in a way that parents could use to plan their own strategies.

There were instances where knowledge of children's educational experiences and the work they were required to produce was essential if parents were to provide realistic support. Yet the relevant information was given systematically only to parents who attended a particular meeting. If parents did not attend the appropriate meeting, they could, for example, be unaware of the continuous assessment element of subjects taken for GCSE and not realize the significance of the work their children were undertaking.

The skills and flexibility required to present interesting and informative meetings for parents have already been discussed, and more attention also needs to be given to the presentation of written communication. So many of the school handbooks and other documentation for parents gathered during this research were not particularly informative and were written in a style that could by itself discourage parents from making contact: booklets that started with a list of school rules rather than a welcoming note were obvious examples. The intention has to be to produce material which is pitched at the right level, so that parents feel neither patronized nor overwhelmed nor demoralized – and that is a difficult balance to strike.

These findings are particularly disappointing given the recommendations of the Plowden Committee more than 20 years ago that 'parents should be informed about the methods used in school' and that 'homework should be agreed and discussed between home and school' (Plowden, 1967).

Most parents said that they and their children were satisfied with the schools attended; they appreciated a 'welcoming atmosphere' and an 'open door' and felt that staff were responsive to their concerns. However, even when parents endorsed the ethos of schools, it was rare for them to approach staff (or be approached by them) unless there was a problem.

There were parents who helped in classrooms or in other activities contributing to the day-to-day functioning of the school, such as running the school bookshop and accompanying children on school trips. This functional involvement is to be welcomed but cannot substitute for the more deliberate dissemination and discussion of information that will help parents to help their child to learn. The use of the word 'involvement' for a range of such activities has served to obscure the key issues. Schools may have a great many parents providing assistance and see this as a thriving system of parental involvement, whereas very little dialogue or learning by either parents or staff may be taking place. It may be that such functional involvement in a school serves to limit access to information from schools if only those parents who are able and willing to 'service' the school gain insight into the curriculum.

The existing structures for involvement readily produced a division between parents who came into school and who were perceived to be interested in, or indeed to care about, their children and those who were not. The term 'parents' is, in any case, misleading in this context, in that while fathers are undoubtedly involved in some aspects of school life, it is generally the mothers who are expected to (and do) take the major role. While some are eager to do this and indeed thrive on this contact, it is not a realistic option for all. Such expectations may place unreasonable demands on those women who are economically active, who have other children to care for or who wish to spend their time in other pursuits.

All of this points to a need for schools to establish a set of principles and a clear sense of purpose to guide their work with parents. Developing meaningful contact with parents is a demanding task with ambitious aims that are not easily achieved. The aims need to be precisely identified and realistically set within a whole-school approach. They need to be effectively communicated and widely endorsed if they are to avoid the problem frequently found in this research of participants having differing perspectives of the same initiatives. Conveying information in a clear and accessible form is difficult and was done with very little success.

Principles and aims

The evidence presented in this report highlights areas for future action if the issue of contact between parents and schools or services is to be tackled productively. Rather than as a peripheral "extra" or optional activity, work with parents should be viewed as an integral part of the way schools and services function. It should be planned and implemented in a more coherent way than is currently the case in many institutions, and it should be given a higher priority. There is undoubtedly value in introducing discrete schemes to involve some parents in schools, but their impact is lessened and potential benefit decreased if they stand in isolation, rather than as one element of a concerted effort to develop productive contact with all.

Parental involvement should not be concerned simply with getting parents into school. It demands an approach to learning that recognizes and draws on the contribution of the home and sees contact with parents on a variety of matters as fundamental. A climate of real approachability and opportunities for dialogue should prevail. On one level, it means routinely considering parental views and seeking parental responses to what is provided. On some issues this could be accomplished via parent governor surgeries. On others it is a case of drawing on parents individually. On another level, parental involvement means seeing parents as active collaborators in their own children's learning and development, and ensuring that they are well-informed about their children's school lives and clear about ways in which they can work with the school.

The goal for practitioners is to plan their overall strategy for contact with parents and to introduce innovative practice as necessary. The aims of work with parents vary considerably. Some of those identified in this research were:

- to establish effective two-way channels of communication, so that parents and professionals are working together and exchanging views and information;
- to involve parents in tackling difficulties their children are experiencing in school;
- to explain the curriculum to parents, so that they are informed of, and can assist in, their children's activities;
- to enable them to support their children through periods of transition and to learn about the new schools;
- to give the opportunity for parents to become part of the school community, at whatever level they prefer;
- to facilitate parents' involvement in decision-making and the review of school policy;
- to provide practical and emotional support with parenting.

The findings do not show the need for a blueprint for practice to be developed, but rather that schools could usefully consider certain basic requirements and the merits of developing a school policy on some practices. To provide parents with clear and accessible information about their own children's progress and any difficulties they are experiencing, to offer opportunities of working with their own children and of gaining an insight into the curriculum and how it is being taught would require a detailed plan of action from many schools. In formulating such a plan, schools could build on and develop the interest in what happens in schools expressed by the parents interviewed in the course of this study.

There are many opportunities available to involve parents in their children's learning and development and to inform them about what is taking place in school. This obviously takes time, but Winkley (1985) observed that, 'where it has been accepted by staff that ten or so parents' evenings a year are standard practice and are worthwhile, then new staff and parents tend to accept, absorb and develop their tradition'.

Factors influencing effective implementation

Key characteristics of the most positive contacts between home and school include a thoroughly considered rationale with explicit aims, a well-designed and realistic strategy to achieve these objectives, and effective communication to parents. Developing channels for clear and accessible written and verbal communication with parents is crucial. Parents should be informed about, and enter into a dialogue with schools about, new educational initiatives, for example, the National Curriculum. At a time when schools are discussing and clarifying these issues internally, the possible benefits and desirability of drawing parents into the process are clear.

What could superficially appear to be 'good practice', for example, having several parents regularly involved in classes, could on closer scrutiny be seen as of limited value, at least in terms of meeting the stated goals. Parents helping in classrooms will not automatically gain an insight into why and how work is undertaken. If open/consultation evenings are to achieve an exchange of information, then privacy and sufficient time are required, and parents need to be aware of the purpose and the part they are expected to play in the session. If the headteacher has a policy of 'my door is always open', then the meaning, as well as the phrase, needs to be explicitly communicated to parents and the limitations of that access acknowledged. Such individual and *ad hoc* sessions would not be an efficient or productive way of informing parents about the curriculum and teaching methods, for example; a school which seriously wished to achieve this aim would need to develop ways of making such information widely available.

The potential value of a school forum for parents to discuss a variety of educational issues emerged from the interviews. Those studied were poorly attended, but appreciated by those who came. They can be enjoyable, worthwhile events; it must, however, be acknowledged that they will have to overcome entrenched attitudes and will not be a form of involvement wanted by all. Such occasions need to be well advertised, organized and presented, with a list of clearly stated aims. They need to take place in an atmosphere that encourages parents to express freely their views and concerns. If parents are consulted, their views must be taken seriously. Parents will have insights, knowledge and experiences to contribute to the discussions and aid decision-making. There may be schools where forums are inappropriate; there are likely to be more where concentrated efforts would realize considerable long-term gains.

Another factor influencing success is the spirit in which the contact is made by staff, which will reflect underlying attitudes. As was noted earlier, teachers often failed to appreciate the practical problems faced by parents who could not fully participate in planned activities. They did not acknowledge the fact that parents might be unaccustomed to challenging a teacher's perception of what was right for their child or to expressing their opinion on educational matters. Flexibility both in practice and attitude was necessary, even in schemes which were generally well received by parents.

A pleasant and welcoming approach to parents is vital. The mother who was not allowed to hand over cash in school for her child's lunch because it was not in an envelope, and who was made to feel like a naughty child; the parents who arrived in a secondary school on a dark winter's evening and spent more than ten minutes searching for the non-signposted staffroom; and the mother who left open evenings feeling that she was being judged as a parent are all absorbing messages about the institution called 'school' that will adversely influence their response to invitations to participate further.

An additional key to success is targeting resources and information at an appropriate level. Materials made available to parents in the schools in this study did not, on the whole, meet this criterion, and there was a sense in which both parents and children were underestimated. The take-home packs contained resources which people already had at home, which were unappealing or whose use was unclear. The Starting School packs were enjoyed, but very few activities were as unfamiliar to the recipients as was supposed by those preparing them; it was too often assumed by teachers that parents would not be able to 'understand' educational principles and practices, even if these were clearly and concisely articulated.

The role of resources in the implementation of work with parents needs careful consideration, and the developments studied have covered the spectrum; some initiatives have been instigated through a specific allocation of resources and others represent a modification of every-day practice. There are clearly some elements of contact that require a substantial financial commitment, and their development will depend on the priorities established in LEAs and schools. The home–school reading initiative in primary schools, for example, required books and other materials, and staff time. The home visiting that featured in some of the schemes chosen for case-study work was accomplished by the creation of a specific post, or by providing replacement teachers for staff undertaking such work. Training staff to develop work with parents and enabling them to draw on the work of colleagues in other settings have resource implications, and the need for both was evident from this research.

Some decisions about the best way to organize developments need to be taken at local authority level. It may be desirable to form clusters of schools in one area or of all schools catering for a certain age group in an authority, so that they can work together in developing an initiative involving parents. In the home–school reading initiative in primary schools, there were common elements that could have been pooled, and schools could have drawn on each other more. A reluctance to 'standardize' provision will be counter-productive if it limits the extent to which common aims can be pursued such as the preparation of materials and booklets or the pooling of experience in running meetings for parents.

It is vital that any practices are regularly and systematically reviewed taking account of the views and experiences of parents as well as staff, to identify any modifications required. There was little evidence that a critical assessment of practice was taking place. This research has highlighted situations where work undertaken with parents came nowhere near to meeting the stated aims, and considerable effort seems to have been expended to little effect.

The way forward

There are a number of ways in which schools and services could progress in their work with parents. Some will undoubtedly continue to develop *ad hoc* approaches to parents with varying degrees of success. Others may have the opportunity to consider fully their provision and plan a way forward that addresses both routine contact and innovation.

This capacity for planning, implementing and reviewing work with parents requires not only a commitment to this practice, but the necessary time and support. Some of the developments included in this study were resourced specifically to foster contact between professionals and parents. However, much of the work depended on the initiative and goodwill of individuals.

Potential changes in practice have to be set in a wider context since they have implications for changing priorities in the education service as a whole. Allocating time for whole-school discussions of current practice with parents, future development and potential innovations would require a firm commitment from headteachers. They have a crucial role to play in determining the ethos of their school and the stance taken with parents. They can provide inspiration and continuity and facilitate a variety of contacts with parents. They can 'set the tone' as well as influence practice. As schools become more financially autonomous under the Local Management of Schools element of the Education Reform Act 1988, local authorities will be less able to offer support to them, and it will fall on headteachers to ensure that work with parents is adequately resourced and prioritized, despite the fact that there will obviously be a number of competing demands on resources and on teachers' time.

Much of the work undertaken with parents has not emerged from a well-defined and considered strategy underpinned by an explicit philosophy. Little enough thought has been given to what enhanced contact between professionals and parents could ultimately result in. Defining and explaining school policy to parents, where it exists, is not easy and may lead to the public overhaul of practices based on what have been considered unalterable facts. Such developments are potentially threatening and require a considerable re-thinking of the position of parents in the functioning of schools. This could be a situation where parents and staff were collaborating regularly on a range of issues and where established practices and attitudes would be under threat. To develop an effective dialogue that was routinely exploited would necessitate substantial changes in attitude and levels of participation on the part both of parents and staff. A great deal of the work being developed with parents does not address these more profound issues, thereby avoiding challenge to current practices and preconceptions.

The findings also highlighted the value of establishing teams of permanent staff with responsibility for disseminating developments in parental involvement to schools and for providing INSET, support, ideas and motivation. Such a support system would help to overcome some of the factors identified as barriers during this study. The team could offer evidence and insights in relation to work with parents, their perceptions of other schools' experiences and expertise in community languages, as required. They could assist in the review and evaluation process that was so necessary in developing effective practice. The use of such personnel as replacement teachers, however, is both expensive and an inefficient use of their valuable skills and experience.

There is a need for in-service training in the practicalities of working with parents, some of it at the level of social skills and presenting information to groups of adults. Enabling schools to identify their aims in consultation with parents and to develop strategies for attaining them would be valuable INSET activities. There is also need for training or information for staff that ensures that they are aware of recent research. The negative responses from some staff to the notion of working with parents in their children's reading and the lack of a systematic approach in most schools sit uneasily with the evidence there is about the value of involving parents in this aspect of the curriculum.

Similarly, advisory teachers can provide the impetus and support to sustain developments. It is vital that their role is supportive, while offering the opportunity to reflect critically on practice; INSET sessions attended during this research sometimes reinforced limited expectations and experiences of work with parents that were not challenged by those running the sessions. The INSET provided should inform teachers of the range of activities possible under the parental involvement umbrella, give them details of what has already been undertaken and challenge assumptions and attitudes that limit future developments.

Work with parents is time-consuming and demanding if it is undertaken to any significant degree, and staff need time and support to carry out the tasks involved. Tizard et al. (1988) made the point that at the current level of resourcing, non-contact time in infant schools is seen as 'pie in the sky', which indicates the low priority given to the allocation of time to develop or plan new initiatives. This research has demonstrated the need for a time allocation for work with parents to be available across the age range, and for practical and motivating support to be available. Work with parents needs to become a key element in the school system, incorporated into the changes brought about by the National Curriculum, acknowledged by senior staff and seen as a worthwhile use of time. Schools are working in a climate of dramatic change and need to respond to a variety of initiatives. To ensure progress, work with parents must either be built into practice (which would require policy directives) or specifically resourced.

Some initiatives are simply not possible without additional resourcing in terms of personnel and materials; others need an injection of training and continuing back-up if they are to thrive. The potential benefits of developing contact between parents and schools or services are, as yet, untapped. A commitment of time, effort and energy that maximizes the potential for enhancing the contact with parents now enshrined in the legislation is required from practitioners and from those who resource and support them both at a local and national level.

Appendix A
The Survey Data

Introduction

A summary of the information obtained from the three questionnaires sent to all the local education authorities in England and Wales (one to the Chief Education Officer/Director of Education and two to advisers/inspectors) is presented here. As could be anticipated, there was variation in the amount of detail provided in response to the questions and on the thoroughness of the replies. However, the responses to these three documents provided an indication of the action being taken both at the LEA and school level to encourage the development of work with parents.

The surveys

Parental involvement at authority level – working parties

Fourteen authorities provided information about working parties which had been established specifically to examine and extend work with parents in schools. A further nine stated that they had working parties which were considering parental involvement as part of a wider brief.

Documentation

Eight authorities were said to have produced, and a further seven to be in the process of producing, documentation relating to parental involvement. All of the documents were unequivocal in their view that the involvement of parents was of considerable benefit. Of the eight, the first comprised a set of points entitled 'Guidelines for home and school', copies of which went to all schools, and to all parents of school-age children in the authority. This A4 sheet detailed the responsibilities of the school, the parents and the pupils.

Two of the eight respondents gave details of authority statements for schools. One of these expressed a firm commitment to community education which was promoted in numerous booklets and leaflets. This detailed document outlined a considerable number of activities designed to involve parents in schools and guidance on how to implement them. The second authority produced a series of documents for infant and nursery teachers on working with parents, giving guidance on such matters as producing written materials for them.

The remaining five authorities submitted reports on parental involvement that had been prepared for Education Committees or subcommittees. These reports identified strategies that could be introduced to develop parental involvement, mostly requiring financial support at authority level. There was, however, one that urged headteachers to consider their own policies and practice in consultation with their staff and parents. LEA suggestions included:

(a) 'to initiate a programme of in-service education suitable to the needs of parents, headteachers, teachers and nursery nurses' (NNEBs);
(b) 'to be aware of current developments and research in this area of work, and to disseminate and refer to such information as appropriate'; and
(c) 'to establish and develop parental support programmes in primary schools'.

Post-holders responsible for parental involvement

All authorities were asked to provide details of any professionals with particular responsibility for developing work with parents; 46 authorities named such a person. Sixteen authorities had given responsibility for parental involvement to the advisers for nursery/primary/early years, as part of their brief, although in six of these they shared it with other professionals, including general advisers, subject advisers and assistant education officers.

In ten authorities the responsibility for parental involvement had been given to other advisory staff, and in four it rested with education officers. With one exception, however, it was not possible to determine whether these responsibilities were actually written into the individuals' job descriptions. There were five authorities where members of the school psychological service were named, and six where parental involvement was said to be the general responsibility of a category of staff, for example, headteachers. In the remaining five authorities naming personnel responsible for this work, there was a greater degree of diversity. One authority, for example, had appointed five advisory headteachers with responsibility for the early years, and parental involvement was regarded as an important part of their brief.

Parent governors

At the time of this survey, the legislative requirement was that (with certain exceptions) every governing body had to have two parent governors (Education Act 1980). The Education (No. 2) Act 1986 altered this requirement, in that the number of parent governors was increased. Authorities were asked to provide information on the number of parent governors recommended for each governing body, and it was of interest to note that 13 of them gave a number above the minimum recommendation.

Authorities were also asked to give details of the number of governing bodies chaired by parent governors. More than half of them stated that there were schools in their authority that had parents in these positions. It was worth noting that nearly one-fifth of those responding to this question had more than ten per cent of these bodies chaired by parent governors.

Formal participation of parents

Authorities were asked about formal participation by parents in the local education system, and more than one-quarter sent details of at least one example. Half of them had a parent representative with full voting rights on the Education Committee. There were eight authorities where parents sat on Appeals Com-

mittees which dealt with school admission. One Parent Consultation Committee consisted of parent governors and was
established to provide a forum to discuss broad issues of educational policy and put forward views to the authority. In
another large authority, 12 District Liaison Committees were
consulted on broad educational matters and they each had two
parent representatives with voting rights (one each from the
primary and secondary sector).

Parental involvement in the pre-school and primary years – involvement of parents in their children's reading

Information about developments in reading was provided by a
large majority of respondents. There were large-scale schemes
specifically to encourage home–school reading of some kind in
only eight authorities; these were schemes initiated by the local
authority in a number of schools. They had a title and were
monitored in some way. In one authority, a home–school reading scheme was organized and supported by advisers in 82
schools. Developing home-reading work was one aspect of
other large-scale initiatives in a further two authorities.

The prevalent pattern was of diverse provision which had
developed in an *ad hoc* way. There were 42 authorities where
paired reading* was said to be used to varying degrees, and 12
where the term *shared reading*† was given. Overall, a substantial
number of schools in 44 authorities were said to be involved in
some kind of home–school reading. Eight respondents said that
this work with parents was developing rapidly in their area.

Involvement of parents with their children in other areas of the curriculum

Slightly fewer respondents forwarded details of developments of
this kind. As in the previous section, the general picture was
one of uncoordinated, *ad hoc* developments, and the responses

---

* 'Paired reading' is commonly used to describe an approach to reading
where adults and children initially read simultaneously and the child
gradually takes the lead (Topping, 1985).
†'Shared reading' is commonly used to describe adults and children reading a
book together.

gave an indication of the range of work currently in progress. One feature of note was that 34 authorities were said to have schools where workshops for parents were held. One authority had established workshops to 'demystify the curriculum' in approximately 60 schools in 1979/80. More usually, workshops were organized on the initiative of individual schools. The pattern was one of growth, as most initiatives were fairly recent, and expansion was noted by several respondents, for example: 'There have been Maths for Families workshops established in many schools since 1986 and the number is increasing all the time.' The majority of workshops were concerned with maths, although a variety of curriculum areas were covered, including computer work, dance, home economics and pre-school learning activities.

General involvement in schools

Most respondents gave examples of general developments and a wide range of work was reported. There were several authorities where classes for parents had been established in schools. One was reported to have Open University study groups in between ten and 20 schools and to have several English as a Second Language classes in operation.

One in three authorities stated that parents helped in schools in a variety of ways. Some responses stated that this help had been formalized through the use of a volunteer register or such initiatives as an 'Extra hands project'. This help included assisting with pupils with special educational needs, running the pantomime, painting the school building, giving talks about their work and running after-school leisure clubs for pupils.

A similar proportion of authorities was reported to involve parents in the transition to school, and there were references to a variety of home–school link initiatives. One authority had about 30 home-link volunteers who made contact with the parents of new entrants. This scheme had been in operation since 1980, and the volunteers were parents of children already in school.

The response of one authority with a range of initiatives indicated the forms that work with parents could take. Their list included home visits for new entrants, parent and toddler meetings, English language classes, parent support groups and parent/teacher/governor working parties to develop curriculum objectives which contributed to the authority guidelines.

Other forms of contact with parents

One-third of respondents gave details of other current contact with parents. There were some references to meetings for parents to explain school policy and different areas of the curriculum, and some to workshops held for parents. Other developments mentioned included parents spending one day a week sitting alongside their child in the classroom, an annual open week devoted to a curriculum area, open evenings to demonstrate the science and technology taught and initiatives to develop work with ethnic minority families.

Developments that have ceased

Respondents were asked to provide brief details of any activities that had been curtailed. Several reported the demise of some work with parents and lack of funding was the predominant reason given. In some areas, parent and toddler groups had been disbanded and parents' rooms reclaimed because of an increase in the school's population and the resulting demand for additional classroom space.

Plans for relevant developments

Respondents were asked to give brief details of any plans to develop work with parents in their authority. One-third provided details of specific plans which were under consideration in their area.

A few authorities were in the process of attempting to increase the number of staff who work specifically with parents. Areas within schools for parents to use were being developed by two authorities, and in a third the parents of pre-school children were being encouraged into schools with the setting up of mother and toddler groups and the expansion of pre-school work with parents, staffed by nursery nurses. Two respondents reported that they were seeking to expand the role of parents in the curriculum.

In two authorities, publications for parents were planned, while other authorities were seeking to improve their in-service support for teachers in their work with parents, particularly in the areas of reading and mathematics. The major development outside schools was the establishment of Family Centres,* and plans to develop these were reported by six respondents.

Staffing: posts of responsibility in schools

Nearly one-half of the respondents said that posts of responsibility had been given for this work in some schools, although this was commonly on a small scale. There were two large, urban authorities where substantial numbers of such posts had been established. In one of these, approximately 60 Scale 2† appointments had been made, and in another, 127 schools had been allocated an extra teacher at Scale 2 or 3 — part of whose brief was to develop home–school links. The majority of posts were made at Scale 2 and most authorities reported only one or two such posts.

Concerning LEA posts to develop work with parents, just under one-half of the respondents said that posts had been established outside schools to facilitate work with parents. Twenty-two authorities had home–school liaison teachers (HSLTs) in post. One, for example, had eight Scale 2 HSLTs to work with pre-schoolers in their homes. Another had 36 part-time Scale 1, eight Scale 2 and one Scale 3 HSLTs, whose brief was to develop activities involving parents in school and to link home and school.

A total of 197 posts as HSLTs were referred to. Of these, nearly half were appointed on Scale 1, and only six were on Scale 3 or above. The range for the number of these posts in each authority was from one part-time to 45 full-time posts. Two large authorities had substantial teams — in one case, of 35 staff.

A few authorities employed educational home visitors or community liaison teachers. There was one parental involvement team, headed by an adviser and employing three Scale 3 teachers and a nursery nurse, and six advisory headteachers were said to be developing this work as part of their brief in one authority. There were several references to Portage work

* Centres providing daycare for pre-school children and support for their parents; they vary substantially in their aims and practice.
† Post of responsibility prior to the introduction of the Main Professional Grade and Incentive Allowances in April 1988.

(see page 163), including one where 20 nursery nurses had been appointed, with a part-time commitment to this form of work with parents.

Schools with parents' rooms/areas

Most respondents reported that there were parents' rooms or areas in some of their schools; most of those with such accommodation provided a figure for the approximate number of schools having this facility. There was some variation in the extent to which space was available in schools for this purpose, although nearly one-half of the authorities had space in five per cent or less of their schools.

Designated community schools

All authorities were asked to give details of any designated community schools in their areas, what activities schools would be involved in to be so designated and any specific resources made available to community schools. Nearly one-third of respondents stated that they had community primary schools (details of secondary schools are given on page 159) and they reported a total of 173 such schools in all. One of these authorities had 35 schools designated in this way (40 per cent of the total number of primary schools), another had 16 and another eight but, in most areas, only one or two schools had been designated.

When respondents identified why a school would be designated in this way, the emphasis was on the use of premises. Most schools provided space for a variety of groups including evening classes, youth clubs, pre-school playgroups, over-60s luncheon clubs and recreational classes. A few philosophical statements were made about the functions of these schools, including "general attitude to parents and community" and "active participation in the lives of parents and the wider community".

Designation in this way attracted extra staffing in eight authorities, additional allowances in 14 authorities and other resources or facilities in most instances. The extra staffing ranged from an extra half-time teacher in three authorities to a situation where each of the three community schools in one authority had an extra community tutor, a home–school teacher and a clerical assistant. Six of those with additional allowances referred to a payment for the headteacher and one to an annual lump sum.

Training courses

Respondents were asked about any training courses specifically concerned with parental involvement that had been run in their authority for any of a variety of audiences. Nearly one-half of them reported at least one course on this topic. The main recipients of the training had been teachers. There were four courses specifically for parents, and six for parent governors. There were two examples of joint sessions for parents and professionals. Five respondents made general statements about the priority given to work with parents in the courses organized for teachers.

Parental involvement in secondary schools – involving parents in reading with their children

Parents were said to be involved in this aspect of the curriculum with their own children in one-half of the authorities. No large-scale schemes were reported, and the largest number of schools undertaking this sort of work in any one authority was five. Brief details of work in 93 schools were provided and two respondents stated that only a few or some schools in their authority were involved. Where information was available about when this work with parents had been established, it was clear that most of it had begun recently; indeed, there were very few examples of developments before 1980.

Paired reading was reported to be undertaken in 20 schools, spanning 13 authorities. Of the remaining 73 schools, 42 had a home–school reading programme and 31 engaged in more general parental contact. It could reasonably be anticipated that much of the work with reading with secondary-age pupils would focus on those experiencing difficulties, certainly as far as paired reading was concerned. In fact respondents from 24 authorities stated that such pupils were involved. Between them, they listed 42 schools where pupils with special needs had been selected for this approach.

Involving parents in other areas of the curriculum with their children

There were few reported instances of parents working directly with their own children in work other than reading. One school had just established a course on craft, design and technology, and another had been holding curriculum workshops since 1983 where parents were encouraged to work alongside their own children. Two special schools in one authority had involved parents in Makaton (sign language) training and conductive learning* since 1985, and another school had instigated a maths project for parents and pupils in the same year.

General involvement in schools

Respondents were asked about the activities undertaken by parents in schools in their authorities. Nearly all provided details of this general involvement and most of them answered a 'follow on' question that enquired about particularly innovative work.

Parents assisting in schools

Nearly one-third of authorities reported that parents assisted in schools, and most of them said that parents regularly helped in the library. A few authorities said that a small number of schools depended on parents for carrying out administrative and office duties.

Parent–teacher associations

These groups have traditionally been regarded as a source of funds, and the quarter of authorities mentioning them indicated their importance in this respect; there was one instance where a cottage had been bought and equipped for outdoor pursuits with the proceeds of such fund-raising; in some schools their activities have spread beyond this. For example, in one school representatives of the PTA visit parents of all incoming first-year

* A specialized programme to enhance the development of children with cerebral palsy.

children and follow this up by arranging daytime meetings in school to bring teachers and new parents together.

Out-of-school activities

Twenty-five authorities commented on the role of parents in out-of-school activities, and a range of ventures was mentioned including an art club, bookshops, stationery shops and music and computer clubs. The most frequently mentioned activity of this sort was that of sport, where ten authorities had schools which had enlisted parental help. A few authorities commented on the role of parents in drama in schools.

Helping in teaching situations

One-third of authorities gave examples of schools where parents with specific expertise contributed to the curriculum. Some home economics departments invited parents to contribute to child care lessons and other teachers had compiled registers of parents' skills and interests which could be drawn on.

Eleven authorities reported that some of their schools regularly invited parents to talk about career options. Parents are also involved in mock interviewing with pupils (11 authorities) and in providing practical help in finding work-experience placements (13 authorities). Three authorities referred to schools where parents from minority cultures and religions came to talk about their traditions. Fourteen authorities reported a total of 17 schools where parents gave reading support, usually in the form of volunteering to listen to pupils with reading difficulties.

Communicating with parents – general meetings

Consultation evenings and open days were frequently mentioned by respondents. Two authorities stated that many of their schools were working to change the nature of such events, to involve and inform parents about educational innovations, as well as keeping them up to date with their children's work. Several authorities gave details of meetings which were intended to extend parental knowledge of more general educational topics and issues relating specifically to the 11–18 age group.

Parental support groups

A few examples of such groups were reported. A Catholic school ran a support programme for the parents of non-Catholic pupils, while another school used the Open University short course on 'Parents and Teenagers' as the starting-point for its support group. Parents and staff established a group in one school, because of their concern about the use of drugs and cigarettes by pupils, to offer mutual support if problems arose. Three authorities gave details of individual schools running support programmes for the parents of children with special educational needs. In one school, a rehabilitation programme had been initiated for pupils with learning and/or behavioural difficulties which brought together the children and their parents, teachers and workers from a Family Centre.

Parents in classes

In many schools, parents were encouraged to join pupils in class. Several authorities reported that there were schools with parents on examination courses alongside their fifth- and sixth-year pupils, although two mentioned that they were disappointed by the low rate of uptake.

Courses and meetings for parents on the curriculum

More than one-third of authorities stated that schools ran courses or workshops to extend parental knowledge and understanding of the curriculum. These ranged from one-off events through to a series of general workshops on the secondary syllabus. One school had a series of workshops on the new GCSE syllabus. There were also courses on subject areas, including maths and science; in addition, a large number of 'back to school' events were reported, including opportunities for parents to experience group work and child-centred learning and to spend time participating in and observing lessons. In one school, parents were invited to follow a teacher during a normal day's teaching; in another, all parents of third-years were welcome to accompany their children through one morning a year in school.

Parental involvement at secondary transfer

Frequent reference was made to meetings for parents of children who had accepted a place at a school. These meetings usually covered the school's aims and its organization and routines, as well as its expectations. In one school, a home–school liaison teacher visited feeder primary schools to establish a contact with parents that was maintained during the period of transfer; and in another, a video had been made for parents of new entrants. One school set aside a week and invited the parents of all prospective first years to join existing first-year pupils in class.

Plans to develop work with parents

All respondents were asked to provide details of any plans to involve parents in schools. One-third gave details of school-based activities, and the emphasis was on involving in some way parents in the curriculum. A range of workshops and meetings for parents was said to be planned. A few authorities gave details of plans to hold meetings for parents to explain school procedures and provide a forum for the discussion of new developments and current issues. In one school, an open evening was intended to give parents details of the self-assessment system operating in a science department; and in another, a series of classes was planned for parents on subjects being taught to their children. A few schools were planning similar 'taster classes', two of them related to GCSE courses.

Details of plans to establish parents' groups were given by several authorities. In one LEA, a school–PTA liaison group concerned with developing the curriculum was to be established alongside one already dealing with industrial and commercial issues. One authority reported that all its secondary schools were to establish working parties (which would include parents) to produce school brochures. Two authorities were about to introduce pupil profiling and intended to involve all parents of secondary school pupils in the process.

Developments that have ceased

Nearly one-third of respondents gave details of work with parents that had ceased. The effects of the teachers' pay dispute in 1985–87 were most commonly given as a reason why work had stopped. The loss of members of staff most actively involved and a lack of parental interest in some activities were also mentioned. The work described included an O-level French course for parents, involvement in work experience placements, volunteer reading assistance, the provision of courses and sports and music activities.

Community secondary schools

Respondents were asked to indicate whether any of the secondary schools within their authority had been designated community schools. In two authorities, all schools had been so designated; another had 27 and one other had 21 community schools; and a further 29 authorities had community secondary schools, with the number of such schools in each authority ranging from one to nine.

The most commonly mentioned community services were adult education, offered either within or separate from mainstream classes, and open access to the schools' buildings, facilities and equipment. Some respondents made reference to a range of youth work, community service, outreach educational opportunities, adult literacy and numeracy programmes and to a general school ethos which promoted the ideal of lifelong education for all members of the local community.

As a result of their designation, community schools had attracted additional resources in terms of staffing, allowances and facilities. One-third of authorities referred to the creation of new posts, which included community tutors, additional deputy headteachers, wardens and clerical staff.

Several respondents referred to a proportion of the time of existing teaching staff being allocated to community education and to establishing links with parents and other community members. The staff concerned usually received additional salary allowances, though it was stated in one authority that allowances tended to vary with the size of the school and in another that the allocation of additional funding was often 'patchy and haphazard'. Mention was made of a home tuition allowance and of funding to provide teaching and ancillary staff cover when the buildings were being used for community activities at weekends.

Additional facilities in the form of purpose-built premises for community use had been provided in a few authorities, as had extra sports facilities and purpose-built youth centres. Other resources included converted or extended buildings, parents' rooms with crèche facilities and adult common or education rooms.

Posts

Authorities were asked to provide details of any posts of responsibility that had been created in schools specifically for work with parents and of any other posts that had been established for work with parents. Seventeen replies contained details of schools where such responsibility lay with senior teaching staff, and another 14 referred to specific posts based, for the most part, in individual schools.

The 17 general responses referred to schools where the head-teacher, deputy and a head of year or a head of department took responsibility for home–school links and for liaison with parents. In contrast, however, the reply from one authority with no such posts contained the following comment from a head-teacher: "I have not given formal responsibility to any teacher for work with parents. I think that the effect of doing so would probably lessen the effect of what we achieve now."

The details of the 14 specific posts demonstrated some variety, although only one respondent referred to posts which were not school-based. In one authority, a school with a very high proportion of Asian pupils had appointed an Asian Community Liaison teacher on Scale 3, while a school with a similar intake had appointed an additional teacher with responsibility for English as a second language to enable more home contacts to be made with ethnic minority families. In the same authority, three other schools had additional members of non-teaching staff (funded from Section 11* monies) who worked with parents. A few respondents referred to schools with home–school liaison posts. These were mostly on Scale 2 or 3 and there were only a few in each authority.

Training courses

Respondents were asked to provide details of any training courses undertaken in the past five years pertaining to work

* Funding for work with ethnic minority families established in Section 11 of the Local Government Act 1966.

with parents. Thirty-two respondents reported some element of such training, either at school or authority level. The majority of courses were either specifically for parent governors or for all school governors, including parent governors. This training was most commonly a series of seminars or lectures on the role of governing bodies. Five authorities organized courses or sessions specifically for parent governors, and one of them had also started a pilot scheme of training based on cascade methods.

Discussion

The data collected from these surveys provide a 'snapshot' of practices involving parents and an indication of their prevalence. It was clear that LEAs varied considerably in the level and type of resources and strategies they employed to develop this work, even allowing for differences in their size. There was variation in who was given responsibility for developing parental involvement in the authority, the proportion of their time allocated to it, the resources made available and the opportunities for parents to contribute to educational policy.

A few statements of intent regarding work with parents were declared at an authority level, but very little evidence emerged of direct guidance or policy statements for schools. The data collected from the detailed work in the 11 schools, schemes and services highlighted the complex and demanding nature of developing contact between home and school. Mortimore and his colleagues (1988) suggested that if local authorities had a clear policy on parental involvement, many of the problems that can arise would be predicted and avoided and the work would be given status. That view is supported by the present research. There was little evidence that authorities were moving towards the Code of Practice described by Mortimore's team. This would specify the roles and conduct of teachers and parents and lay down procedures to be followed in the event of disagreements.

The two surveys of practice in schools have identified pockets of innovation and growth that have two major implications. One is that schools and services varied dramatically in their attitude and approach to parents and in what they provided for them; the other is that the need to disseminate descriptions and evaluations of practice is of paramount importance. There were clear instances of well-established, highly regarded practices in some settings that were deemed unworkable in others, and yet which may well have transferred successfully. These developments included home-link volunteers for families whose children were about to start school, support groups of a variety of kinds for parents, and parental involvement in policy and decision-making in schools. Declarations that "it would not work here" require rigorous scrutiny informed by an awareness of practice in other establishments.

There was considerable variation noted in the type of information available to parents from schools and the way it was communicated. Again, there were standard practices in some schools that would appear extremely innovative in other settings; for example, having one day a week on which parents were invited to sit alongside their children in class.

Without a clear policy statement or a coordinated approach, work with parents almost inevitably emerged as an 'extra' and was particularly vulnerable in terms of resources. There was very little accommodation available for parents in schools, and the extent to which designated staff were available to establish and develop work with them was extremely variable.

The lack of a clear policy or rationale at school level hampered progress. The data collected from the detailed work in schools highlighted lost opportunities and the frustrations of parents and staff when aims and objectives were unclear. Sufficient evidence is available to support an investment in parental involvement that is widespread but tailored to individual schools' circumstances. This would cover periods of transition (starting and transferring school), parental assistance in classrooms, involvement in reading and other aspects of the curriculum, and opportunities to discuss and contribute to school policy and practice.

The highly regarded and well-formulated pockets of innovative practice with parents and the clear lines of communication evident in some settings may act as a source of inspiration and ideas for those who wish to develop contacts between home and school. Clear statements of intent and more uniformity in provision would be of value to the innovators and enable others to follow suit. There is no standard package that should apply across the board, but there are serious discrepancies in the breadth, content and quality of service available to parents, and in the support available to staff, in the present situation.

Appendix B
The Studies of Parental Involvement

Newborough LEA's Early Years Support Team – a pre-school team working with children with special educational needs

This team is part of the educational provision of a small, urban LEA and works in a socially mixed area, mostly with white families. Nearly ten years ago the authority's School Psychological Services, in conjunction with other representatives from the education department, social services and the health authority, carried out a survey of the provision for pre-school children with special needs and their families. By the time the survey was completed, a number of Portage* schemes had been established, as had Hester Adrian programmes for Down's Syndrome children (Mittler and Mittler, 1982). Parents in Newborough, included in the survey, were keen to take part in such a scheme, confirming the views of the professionals that this type of support was what parents wanted.

It was proposed that there should be a team of teachers who would work with parents and children at home on the principle of 'assessment through teaching', as in the Portage system. The team consists of four qualified teachers, one of whom is designated the head of service. At the time of the study, they were working with 60–70 families on a regular basis.

* Portage takes its name from a town in Wisconsin, USA, where the system of teachers visiting parents with pre-school children with special educational needs at home, to suggest ways in which they could assist their own children's development, was first developed (Daly et al., 1985).

To be referred to the team, a child must have a special educational need, as defined within the terms of the Education Act 1981, and the parents must agree to the referral. Most referrals are made by the Senior Clinical Medical Officer as a result of routine assessment checks at six months, 18 months or three years. A growing number of children are referred by hospital doctors and paediatricians soon after a birth where a handicap has been diagnosed. A few referrals are made by health visitors, educational psychologists and heads of nurseries.

After a referral has been made, the Early Years Support Team determines whether the difficulty experienced by the child is educational and assesses whether the team is the appropriate agency to deal with it. All the initial visits are made by the head of service, who makes an assessment of each child's needs. A vital part of this visit is to obtain from parents as full a picture of the child as possible. After this visit, the team works regularly with 60–70 per cent of children and another 10–20 per cent will be given a further appointment, even if it is just for one return visit some months later.

As well as providing parents with ideas for activities and strategies to use with their children, it is hoped that the teachers will get to know the families with whom they work and be able to offer other support as required. It is a policy of the team, however, that no one teacher works with a family for more than 18 months (it may be 12 months where older children are concerned). In this way, the children learn that they have different teachers at different times in their lives, parents are encouraged not to become dependent on one person and staff work with a broad cross section of children and families.

An important part of the team's work is the way they involve parents in the review procedure, including the writing of reports, as the children approach school age. The intention is to place parents on equal terms with the professionals who have been involved with their children. Parents are encouraged to present their accounts of their children's progress. Teachers on the team are important links with nurseries and reception classes, and they also accompany staff from these settings into the home, or provide cover while the staff go to meet prospective pupils and their parents.

The team has also provided workshops and short courses for parents and it recently gave a great deal of support to the establishment of a Parents' Representative Group.

Summary, sample and method

This is an example of a service which is concerned to support parents in their homes, to help them develop skills which they can use with their children and to encourage them to participate actively in the decision-making processes in relation to these children. It undertakes a particular type of contact with an identified group of parents and is staffed and resourced specifically for this purpose.

Twenty-two of the families being supported by the pre-school team were approached for interview and 19 agreed to take part. The head of the service, the three permanent members of the team and a teacher seconded to the team for a year were also interviewed. Team members were accompanied on home visits, and staff meetings and parents' meetings were attended.

Dalebridge Nursery School's Family Support Project

This nursery school has 160 children on roll, about half of whom attend in the morning and half in the afternoon, and they usually enter the nursery during their fourth year. The school is located in a densely populated, urban area in a large LEA. It serves a predominantly working-class, white population, although about one-fifth of the pupils are Asian. It is staffed by a headteacher and deputy headteacher, one full-time and two part-time teachers, and three full-time and two part-time nursery nurses. In addition, there is an educational home visitor (EHV) who is also a qualified teacher.

In the early 1980s, the LEA invited schools to submit proposals for new schemes to be considered for Urban Aid funding. This nursery school requested, and was granted, money for a Family Support Project and, as a result, the EHV was appointed. The funding paid for this worker for 12 hours a week during term-time and for four hours a week during eight weeks of the holiday period, as well as providing a lump sum of several hundred pounds, and the promise of £100 for each of the following four years, for materials. Charitable funding was secured locally for further resources. The funding has recently been taken over by the LEA. The two main strands of the EHV's work are home visiting and pre-nursery groups.

Home visiting

The EHV visits every potential entrant to the nursery school. Children's names may be registered at the school when they are two and three-quarters and the home visits take place shortly after registration. The visits usually last for about half an hour and provide an opportunity for the parents to hear about the school and to discuss their child and any concerns or queries they may have. In a few cases, long-term visiting is undertaken and, if the EHV is concerned about a child or if a problem is discussed during the visit, the parent and child may be invited to a pre-nursery group.

Pre-nursery groups

There are usually three such groups running each week, but this will be extended to four if there is sufficient demand. About six parents are involved in each group. Meetings are held in a community room housed in a Portacabin in the grounds of the nursery school. Most parents attend for just one term, although there are some who come for longer, and younger siblings are welcomed.

The groups begin with a 'free play' time while the parents watch or play with their children and talk to each other or to the EHV, who is also busy with the children. After a short break for refreshments, the EHV organizes a group session which includes story-telling and singing. The groups are designed to provide an opportunity for children to engage in a range of activities and for parents to draw support from one another and the EHV.

Summary, sample and method

The EHV is a post funded to develop a specific type of work with parents along pre-arranged lines. As a result, information is available about families prior to the child's entry into school, and the school has a facility to offer to parents before a nursery place becomes available.

The pre-nursery groups were attended on several occasions and the EHV was accompanied on home visits. Meetings for parents were also attended including one for the parents of new entrants to the nursery and the Annual Parents' Meeting.* The mothers attending two pre-nursery groups were approached for interview and all but one agreed to take part, resulting in 11 interviews. The headteacher and the educational home visitor were also interviewed.

Lane End Infants – a school with a range of parental involvement

This urban infant school caters for approximately 300 pupils, of whom 80 are part-time and attend the nursery unit. There are approximately ten members of teaching staff. The school serves a socially mixed catchment area and includes some children from professional backgrounds and some from service families. Approximately one-quarter of the pupils are from ethnic minority groups.

Parents are invited to be involved with the school in a variety of ways. The headteacher views contact with parents as a central part of her work and the many forms this takes include: a school policy advisory group, open to everyone and providing an opportunity to discuss school matters; a parents' coffee area and notice-board; and information leaflets on a variety of topics and a twice-termly newsletter.

The school handbook was produced in consultation with parents and contains statements conveying a clear intention to liaise closely with them. The section headed 'Parents' states: 'At our school there is a chance for everyone who wants to become involved to do so and at whatever level they wish. As teachers, we value highly the warm feelings of support from all parents which helps us in our work for the children.'

At the level of general involvement, it is intended that the school policy advisory group meets twice termly and it is described in the handbook as a body that 'helps our school to serve the needs of the children and families by looking critically

* A meeting held by governors for parents, as a requirement of the Education Act (No. 2) 1986.

and constructively at our school procedures and practices'. A series of meetings for parents and teachers to decide how classes should be organized for the next year has been held in school, at which, for example, the options of having larger classes and a 'floating' teacher were aired and discussed.

Also at a general level, parents are invited to attend any school assemblies, to help in classrooms and around the school, and to become involved in the Parents' Association. The information leaflets cover a wide range of topics, including reading, water and sand play and what happens in school during lunchtime, as well as one listing local community organizations and another dealing with child abuse.

At the level of the individual child, the handbook explains that the school is working to build on 'the numerous qualities and skills which you have fostered in your child at home'. Parents are encouraged to discuss their child's progress informally and to enquire about the school's programme of learning. It is stressed that they are 'welcome at anytime at the school'. Some classes have 'take-home' packs of books and games available. The headteacher said that she wants to provide a relaxed and encouraging atmosphere for parents, so that they will want to contribute to the school and will feel able to make the necessary contact about individual children. She wants them to see school as a "worthy place" not just in a narrow sense in relation to the child, but as part of the wider community.

Summary, sample and method

This is a school where the headteacher and some members of staff see contact with parents as a priority. Some innovations have been introduced and the intention is that day-to-day contact should be well managed and productive for the parents concerned. Care is taken to produce attractive and accessible written materials and the ethos is one of drawing parents into school life in whatever way possible.

The parents of approximately one-sixth (n = 53) of the pupils on roll were approached for interview and 44 agreed to take part. Interviews were undertaken with six of the eight permanent members of the teaching staff. In addition, a variety of meetings for parents were attended including those on policy and two Annual Parents' Meetings. There were also informal discussions with staff and parents during visits to the school.

Tatehill First School – an induction programme for starting school

This school caters for approximately 200 children and has a teaching staff of nine. It is situated in an urban area and the children come from a socially mixed community, where the great majority of people are white.

Drawing on research that documented the difficulties children experienced in starting school (Cleave, Jowett and Bate, 1982), an induction programme with several elements that focused on the main areas of discontinuity was devised by the headteacher, one reception class teacher (although it was used in both reception classes) and an educational psychologist. The original idea came from the school and the psychologist was eager to contribute, particularly during a sabbatical year. The headteacher emphasized that development of the programme had been a three-way process drawing on the experience and expertise of the three professionals involved. In addition, there was some support from advisory staff in the authority.

The intention was to extend contact with parents around the period of transition, on the assumption that this would reduce children's initial difficulties in starting school, enable parents to prepare their children more effectively for school and lay the foundations for a good parent–teacher working relationship. The establishment of this partnership with parents was a key concept in the thinking behind the scheme.

The induction programme consists of a video that is shown in school prior to children starting, a second meeting in school prior to entry, a lunchtime and playtime visit for children, an afternoon in the classroom they will be going in to and a set of Starting School packs. There is also a meeting a month *after* the children start.

The Starting School packs

Each pack covers one of five themes, for example, time and colour, and the intention is that each child has the opportunity to work through one pack on each theme. Each includes a story-book, a cassette tape, scissors and materials for developing skills needed in the reception class. There are also suggestions for encouraging social skills, for example, dressing and undress-ing and being sufficiently confident to eat with large numbers of other children, as well as suggestions for playing at home. Particular attention is given to the vocabulary associated with the theme of each pack, with the emphasis on every-day activities and concepts (drawing upon Boehm, 1970). The materials within each pack are interrelated to encourage the association of ideas, and generalizations of skills and memory. The packs allow for repetition and practice to consolidate children's learning. There is a 'Let's remember...' sheet for the child and the parent to complete, which encourages the review of activities (as in the plan-do-review model advocated in the High Scope Curriculum, Weikart, 1971) and provides feedback to the school. Each pack contains a parent–child booklet, which explains to parents how the activities should be tackled, as well as the underlying rationale for what is included. A clear and concise exposition for parents of the 'how and why' of activities is considered to be fundamental to the effective use of the material. The importance of listening to children and of responding to their suggestions is emphasized.

One teacher saw part of the purpose of the packs as a "physical link" that children readily associated with the school they were about to enter and which formed part of the 'ritual' of transition (as outlined by Watt, 1988). The other teacher emphasized the pack's value in helping to "familiarize the child with school activities and expectations".

The video

This was made in school and features those activities within a reception child's day that have been shown to cause most difficulty for new entrants such as lunchtime, playtime and getting ready for physical education lessons. The video also shows a parent and child working through some of the activities in the packs. It gives parents the opportunity to select from the visual scenes those examples that could help their child. The headteacher explained that, "The video puts it across clearly that they *have* to cope on their own, that they have to become independent and confident. That's the most important thing to give a child. That's vital."

The meetings

The first meeting is held on an evening early in the term before the children are due to enter school. It provides an opportunity for parents to see the classroom that their child will be in and to talk to the staff. The headteacher speaks to parents about what they could do to help their children settle in school; the video is shown and the packs are described. It is emphasized that using the packs should be fun and that giving children this individual attention is important. The importance of play in children's development is stressed.

Parents are invited to choose a pack to take home with them and told on which afternoons they can come to school to exchange it; it is intended that they are kept for between one to two weeks. The packs are exchanged by a parent who has received appropriate training, and the teacher who was instrumental in developing them attends whenever possible. The headteacher has contact with parents during these sessions.

The second meeting for parents prior to their children starting school covers practical matters and is held during the day, so that while the headteacher talks with parents, the children spend time in the classroom they will be going to. The third meeting is held one evening about a month after the children have started school. Parents are able to see their children's work and talk about how they are settling in. The meeting also includes a session by both reception teachers on how mathematics and language are taught. Games and activities are on display and parents are invited to ask questions.

Summary, sample and method

The headteacher and two members of staff in this school were keen to change the way the school responded to parents and children during the period of transition and devised a programme to do this. The support of an outside professional added an extra impetus.

All 13 parents whose children started school one term were interviewed, as were the headteacher and the two reception class teachers. Details of the thinking that had led to the scheme were obtained from the educational psychologist. In addition, each part of the induction programme, including the pack exchange days, was attended, for observation of the events and for informal contact with parents and staff.

Millshire LEA's Home–School Reading Initiative

In the mid-1980s, senior members of staff in this large, rural authority became very interested in work undertaken with parents and children in relation to reading, most notably in Haringey (Tizard, Schofield and Hewison, 1982), and were keen to translate this interest into practice. Two primary advisers and two advisory teachers were given responsibility for establishing the scheme. One of the advisers spoke of "staff receptiveness" in schools to this development and advanced her view that "the climate was right". Schools enter the scheme in phases. Twenty took part in the first year and rather fewer join annually. While priority was given to schools in 'disadvantaged' areas in the initial selection, it is anticipated that all schools catering for pupils in the five to eight age range in the authority will be taking part within a decade. The scheme will be available to pupils from a variety of social backgrounds, the large majority of whom will be white.

The central feature of the scheme is that books and games are available for parents and children regularly to share at home. The emphasis is on reading as an enjoyable experience to produce children who can and do read. It is acknowledged that schools vary considerably in their contact with parents about reading, but all staff are expected to inform parents about their school's approach to reading and language development work. It is also anticipated that parents will, with the school's active encouragement, acquire extra skills that will aid their children's development. An adviser described parents as "hungry for activities" and said that there is a "fund of energy and commitment that really needs to be utilized".

Responsibility for the organization and running of the scheme lies with the advisers, and the advisory teachers have a substantial part of their working week allocated to it. A lump sum of several thousand pounds for resources was given to each adviser initially, and a similar sum is available annually to maintain the work. Each school is allocated several hundred pounds' worth of books and games on joining and an annual 'top up' of these resources. In-service sessions are held for staff prior to, as well as after, joining the scheme, and where appropriate supply cover to attend these sessions is available. Most of the schools receive support from an advisory teacher for one session a week for the first two terms. Thus there is a clear financial commitment from the authority in terms of personnel and resources.

The advisory staff have produced booklets relating to the scheme for teachers and parents, and support groups for staff have been established to provide opportunities to share ideas and experiences in each locality.

At its broadest, the scheme involves parents coming into school to work on projects of various kinds with their own children and also taking materials home to use. Schools are at different starting-points and respond to the initiative in very different ways. 'Link' cards, which children take home regularly and which provide space for parents and teachers to write to each other about children's progress, are available, but again, these are used to differing degrees. Staff decide how to present their policy on reading, the age and number of children involved, how to store, organize and catalogue the materials and how to introduce and develop the work with parents. Clearly space is one crucial factor in relation to storage and, more significantly, in determining what work can be undertaken with parents in school. Some schools use their own resources to make accommodation more suitable for parents, for example, by introducing comfortable chairs or soft furnishings. Some teachers are given time to prepare teaching materials for the scheme in school and their classes are covered by colleagues during workshop sessions.

In some schools, several workshops are held each week, with the aim of facilitating parents working with their own children on a one-to-one basis. Some workshops involve projects on a topic, some result in the production of a game and others are more open-ended. Schools vary as to whether younger siblings attend, whether facilities are provided for them if they do and in what is provided for children whose parents do not come. Most of the sessions last for an hour.

Summary, sample and method

This scheme is a large-scale, authority-led and resourced, attempt to involve parents in their children's reading. Schools are given resources and time to support this work and are free to develop it as they choose. What emerges is a range of responses, some more clearly linked than others to the guiding principles outlined by the advisers.

Five schools with well-established workshops were selected. These schools were visited during workshop sessions and 71 questionnaires were distributed to parents. Fifty-five were returned completed, giving a response rate of 77 per cent. The seven teachers directly involved in these workshops were interviewed. In addition, numerous visits were made to schools taking part in the home–school reading initiative, and in-service sessions and support group meetings for teachers were attended, as were introductory meetings for parents. On these occasions, the scheme was discussed with headteachers, teachers and parents.

Stanfield Middle School – a school with a policy of home visiting

This middle school is in an urban setting and has 18 teachers on its staff. It caters for approximately 340 pupils aged from eight to 12 years. About 95 per cent of the pupils are Asian, with parents born in Asia or East Africa. In addition, there are small numbers of Afro-Caribbean and white pupils. Most of the parents are engaged in manual or semi-skilled occupations.

A very high percentage of the Asian pupils are Sikhs and the rest are either Muslims or Hindus. The main Asian language spoken at home is Punjabi, followed by Urdu, Hindi and Gujarati. The previous headteacher is reported to have believed in the 'assimilation' of all minorities, and as part of this philosophy no child was allowed to use any language in the school other than English. It is also said that parents were not usually encouraged to come past the school gate or to participate in school life beyond a minimal level.

The present headteacher is attempting to counter the negative images of the school which he feels have been created. The staff believe that parents want to be involved in schools but are unfamiliar with the idea of such contact, and that patterns of shiftwork mean that they have little time to develop it. There are plans to convert an under-used area in the school into a parents' room to be shared with the First School which is on the same site.

A Parents' Association was formed shortly after the new headteacher was appointed. Some time later, it was replaced by a

Parents' and Friends' Association. Despite the very large proportion of Asian families, the original Association had been dominated by white parents and the functions which it organized were said to be "typically British". More recently, however, there has been a greater involvement in the school and an increased emphasis on functions associated with religious festivals. Parents, other members of the families and of the community are now coming in to celebrate Guru Nanak's birthday, Diwali, Eid, Christmas and Baisaki. For one Christmas concert over 500 tickets were sold.

The school leaflet states that parents are welcome into school at any time and that more formal open evenings take place each term. In addition to these meetings, curriculum evenings are held to give parents information about what is done in school. Very few parents have so far responded to the school's requests for them to come in to work in the classrooms, but it is thought that this will only happen when they have more experience of coming into school on other occasions.

At the time of the research, the school had received a grant of several thousand pounds from the European Commission to extend its work with parents and a list of priorities had been drawn up. These were said by the headteacher to be based on the "attainable", which was seen to lie mainly in the direction of working with parents in the home. The main aims were to improve communication with parents, to develop a welcoming atmosphere in the school and to produce multilingual material for the home.

Before this headteacher came to the school, children had not been allowed to take their reading books home and this was changed. One teacher also visits the homes of all first-year pupils, and has recently been allocated time within the school day for this work. The intentions are that during the visits there will be a discussion of the importance of reading with children and of talking to them in any language, and that parents will be encouraged to come into school and to contact teachers at any time.

Summary, sample and method

In this school, a variety of attempts have been made by staff to improve contact with parents, after a history of very little parental involvement. Many of the parents were not educated in the UK, and as well as providing information on what goes on in school, the headteacher is particularly anxious to show parents that their culture is valued. The work reflects the commitment of the headteacher and some members of staff to develop home links, and some resources have been provided to facilitate some of their plans.

Interviews were conducted with seven members of staff in this school. These were with the headteacher, the deputy head-teacher, the multicultural support service teacher, three form teachers and a part-time support teacher. The parents of one-third of the first year pupils ($n = 21$) were approached for interview and 17 agreed to take part. An experienced inter-viewer, fluent in the relevant community languages, was ap-pointed specifically to undertake the interviews. In addition, members of the team attended a variety of meetings and con-certs in school and accompanied the multicultural support ser-vice teacher on home visits.

Planeborough LEA's Working with Parents Team

Planeborough is an urban authority that includes both industrial working-class areas and a middle-class commuter belt. It has an ethnically mixed population. The team was set up three years ago, to work in schools alongside staff and parents, to facilitate parental involvement. It consists of four teachers seconded to this work for one day a week, for a year, although one member of the team has had an extended attachment.

Five years ago, two primary schools in the authority were designated as Community Schools and the headteachers and staff wanted this to mean much more than merely dual use of facilities. Parents were already involved in a number of different ways in both schools and it was decided to develop a whole-school approach working towards a genuine partnership of parents and teachers. The staff of both schools came together for a series of discussions which were attended by a newly appointed primary inspector and by a member of the authority's Learning Support Team. The Working with Parents Team grew from these initiatives.

Three key areas were identified. The first was home–school liaison, which included setting up home visiting, developing in-duction courses for new parents and improving communication between home and school; the second was to improve the Parent and Toddler Clubs by providing a broader range of activities; and the final one was to develop courses for parents to inform them of what the schools were trying to do and to stress the value of cooperation between parents and teachers.

There is a clear commitment to the idea of parents as partners and to the principle that, after full discussion and negotiation, support should be given to schools to develop activities that staff in those schools feel to be appropriate. The idea of a contract between the team and the school is considered to be very important because school staff and the team must work closely together if initiatives are to continue after the support has ceased. The work which has been supported in schools is very varied but a basic objective has always been that schools should work towards their own whole-school policy of parents as partners and that the expertise which is developed in this area should be shared with teachers in other schools as much as possible.

Summary, sample and method

The team is an example of an authority-supported initiative to help schools develop their work with parents, which depends on annual secondments for its members.

Interviews were conducted with the primary inspector and the four team members who were in post at the time of the fieldwork. Nine headteachers who had been involved with the team were also interviewed.

Seventeen parents of pupils from the fourth year of one of the initiating primary schools were approached to take part in the study and 15 agreed to be interviewed (this represented half of the group year). Ten members of staff from the same school were also interviewed.

Two group discussions were held for 11 parents, who had attended a six-session course on how young children learn in one of the schools receiving support from the team.

In addition, two different types of INSET courses were attended, as well as various meetings for parents.

The Home–School Liaison Committee at Woodvale Comprehensive School

Woodvale is a mixed, 11–18 comprehensive community school with approximately 700 pupils on roll and nearly 50 members of teaching staff. The school serves a mainly working-class, white population in an urban setting. The closure of much of the heavy industry in the area has resulted in high levels of unemployment. The school buildings include a purpose-built youth club and community centre. The school's 12-point philosophy is detailed for parents in the prospectus and includes, 'That the school as a family is an integral part of a wider family, locally, nationally and internationally' and also 'That the education of the child involves an active partnership between school and home'.

The school produces a termly newsletter of 30 or so pages and curriculum statements designed to let parents know what pupils will be studying. A contract has been devised that sets out parents' rights and responsibilities and seeks their assurance that the latter will be adhered to. Literature from the school emphasizes the need for 'as much contact as possible with parents'. The prospectus stresses that parents are welcome in school and that they will be contacted by staff as the need arises, not just through formal parents' evenings. The prospectus also urges parents to contact the school, 'if they have any queries or problems – anytime' and invites them to join in home–school activities. Parents are able to attend classes as students and some volunteer to help children who are experiencing difficulty with their work, or assist with preparing materials.

The development of the committee

In the early 1980s, there was concern about the value of the Parent–Teacher Association since its last two Annual General Meetings had been attended by only 15 and eight parents respectively. It was decided to replace this organization by home–school groups for each of the years one to five. The home–school groups were established to meet twice termly. One meeting is to discuss the report produced on each pupil (there are two minor and one major reports each year), and the other is designed as an opportunity to discuss wider educational issues. The discussion meetings attract a "faithful band", which the acting headteacher estimated to be between eight and 10 per cent of parents. During the course of this study, topics covered in these meetings included option choices for GCSE, records of achievement, how mathematics is taught in school and the implications of the Education Reform Act 1988.

The Home–School Liaison Committee's constitution states that it should comprise four parents from each year elected or re-elected annually, the parent governors, the headteacher and four other members of staff. The Committee meets termly and meetings are minuted. Three officers are elected and, at the time of reporting, all posts were held by parents.

The meetings generally begin with a report from a parent from each year group about the group's most recent meeting for that year. Each year group is usually represented by one or two parents. The headteacher reports on general school matters and there is an opportunity to discuss relevant issues. Parents receive information about the day-to-day running of the school and about future developments and are able to raise any matters of particular concern to them. Matters discussed during the period of fieldwork included concern about the lack of trained first-aid assistance for pupils, the proposed consortium for sixth-year pupils, staff redeployment, why so few parents attended year group meetings and the Education Act 1988.

Summary, sample and method

This Committee provides an opportunity for parents to meet staff and discuss general school matters and policy. The idea evolved in response to concern about low turn-out for the previous Association. Staff attend on a voluntary basis; parent representation is disappointingly low.

Home–School Liaison Committee meetings were attended over a period of a year, as were the discussion meetings of the home–school groups. At least one meeting for each of the years one to five was included. The 13 parents who attended the Home–School Liaison Committee over this period were inter-viewed, as were the six members of staff (including the acting headteacher and two deputies).

Banthorpe Comprehensive School's transition programme for first-year pupils

Banthorpe Comprehensive School is mixed and caters for nearly 800 pupils, aged between 11 and 16, and has just over 50 members of teaching staff. It serves a socially mixed, white, rural community where many children travel to school from nearby villages.

The headteacher states in the school prospectus that, 'The education of children is best achieved through a full partnership between home and school. Therefore I look for as much personal contact between yourself and the school teaching staff as possible.' A newsletter for parents is prepared termly, through which they are informed of ways in which they can become involved in school and are invited to participate. Some parents attend classes in school for their own education.

The headteacher emphasizes that the school has a tradition of extending a welcome to new entrants and this was formalized by the transition programme introduced by one of the heads of department in his capacity as deputy head of House. The school has, for some time, produced a 'Welcome' booklet for first-year pupils which emphasizes the benefits the school has to offer and acknowledges that there may be uncertainty and apprehension at the time of transfer.

The head of department outlined his plans for the transition programme to colleagues, explaining that developing work with parents had been of particular interest to him for some time, 'having experienced the advantages of knowing and involving parents through my work with extracurricular activities and adult education'. During a recent one-year secondment he had had the opportunity to clarify his aims and the induction programme grew out of that.

Children spend a day in school during the term before they start. There are meetings in school for parents before their children start, at the end of their first half-term and during the second half-term. A meeting to discuss individual children's progress is held during the second term. It was intended that parents and children be invited to work on a project at home, but this has not been initiated to date.

The meeting prior to school entry is concerned with providing parents with general information, largely of a practical nature, about how the school functions. Other meetings are more innovative. The letter inviting parents to one meeting held during the first term describes it as an opportunity to '(a) establish a relationship between parents, teachers and children and (b) increase parents' understanding of *some* aspects of the curriculum and teaching methods'. The emphasis is on making contact rather than discussing individual children and on conveying information about what children do in school. The letter adds: 'we feel that it is important for parents, teachers and children to work together and to demonstrate some things which are quite different from parents' own school days.'

The teacher responsible for this programme has clearly identified the aims and objectives of contact with parents during this period and has communicated them to colleagues. The aims include: 'To increase parents' understanding of the curriculum and teaching method used', and 'To demonstrate to children that parents and teachers work togther in partnership with their [the pupils'] interests in mind'. The objectives include: 'Parents will be well known to the form tutor' and vice versa, and 'Parents will have had the opportunity to express their views regarding any aspect of school life'.

Summary, sample and method

In this school, an approach to dealing with children's transfer to secondary school is being developed by an individual member of staff, building on some attitudes and practices already in evidence. He is enthusiastic and keen to motivate colleagues. His secondment was of value, in that it provided the opportunity to clarify aims and develop a theoretical perspective.

A questionnaire was sent to the 25 parents of first-year children in one House and 17 of them returned it, giving a response rate of 68 per cent. The headteacher and the two teachers most directly involved in the programme were interviewed. Each stage of the programme was attended in school when informal contact with staff and parents was made.

Marksbury Community School – a secondary school with parental involvement in GCSE options

This mixed comprehensive school for 11- to 18-year-olds is located at the edge of a city and the catchment area is prodominantly working class. It was recently designated a community college and school.

There are over 1,300 pupils on roll, nearly one-third of whom are from ethnic minority groups, and a staff of approximately 80 teachers. A small number of teachers are involved in the work on the community side, and a wide range of activities are provided for the local population, including a termly newsletter delivered to every home in the area.

The school booklet has recently been substantially revised and a small working party of teachers, parents, governors and community staff was formed to undertake this task. This group canvassed the views of parents about the information they wanted to see in such a booklet and when it was produced they were asked for their opinions. The booklet contains sections on 'Parents in School' and on 'Keeping in Touch with Parents'. Under the heading 'Parents in School', a welcome is extended to all parents to visit the school and talk to members of staff about their children's progress, both at open evenings and at other times. The booklet also gives examples of the variety of ways in which parents participate in the school. Home–school groups (one for each year) were established three years ago to replace the School Association, which had failed to interest many parents. A senior teacher has been given responsibility for coordinating the work with parents and for increasing parental awareness of curriculum developments.

The focus of the research was on how parents of third-year pupils are involved with their children and the teachers in the decisions surrounding GCSE options. Two information leaflets are produced which are intended for pupils and parents. A few parents were selected to comment on these booklets when they were in draft form. Parents are also invited into school on a number of occasions to learn more about the choices available and to discuss them with members of staff. The booklets contain information about choice of subjects and examine issues which it is thought would interest parents, for example, why certain combinations of subjects are not available.

The first booklet is sent home with pupils towards the end of October with a letter inviting parents to a meeting in early November. The second booklet, which contains more detailed information on subjects, is distributed shortly after this event. Parents are then invited to a consultation evening with individual subject teachers at the end of November to discuss children's progress in specific subjects with particular reference to the GCSE course and options. At the beginning of March, parents are again invited into school to meet tutors to discuss the choices which have been made by their children. It is expected that the completed forms indicating individual subjects will have been returned before this meeting, so that decisions can be finalized on that evening.

Summary, sample and method

This scheme involved a series of meetings and related booklets on GCSE options designed to inform parents of, and involve them in, the decisions which face their children. This was a school initiative forming part of a developing policy of contact with parents.

One-tenth of the parents of third-year pupils (n = 23) were approached for interview and 21 agreed to take part. Interviews were also conducted with a deputy headteacher, a teacher with responsibility for parental involvement, the head of the third year and the seven third-year tutors. In addition, a variety of meetings for parents, including those focusing on option choices, were attended.

Overlea Community Comprehensive School – contact with parents around the time of transition, a home–school reading project and local authority support

This school is situated in a small town in a rural area. It serves a white, socially mixed community. It has approximately 630 pupils aged between 11 and 16 and nearly 50 teachers.

Contact with parents at secondary transfer

In mid-October of the year preceding transfer, all prospective parents are invited to a meeting at which the headteacher gives a talk and they are then able to go around the school, visit classrooms and examine work on display.

During the early weeks of the second half of the autumn term, a few members of staff and pupils from this school visit six local primary schools to talk to the parents of prospective pupils. The headteacher is accompanied by one or two senior colleagues and one or two ex-pupils of the primary school who are now in the upper forms of the comprehensive. The head-teacher emphasizes the importance of a smooth transition to school, invites parents to visit Overlea Comprehensive School during the daytime and gives detailed information about the school, including the teaching methods employed, the curriculum followed, the public examination results and the philosophy of the staff, which stresses the importance of the individual. Parents are invited to ask questions of the teachers and pupils.

Parents then come into the secondary school for a meeting in July. The children visit Overlea in the morning and their parents join them in the afternoon. The headteacher speaks about the aims and objectives of the school and the need to prepare pupils for a rapidly changing society. There are short contributions from the head of the first year, from a first-year tutor, and from a representative of the Parent–Teacher Association urging parents to participate and give their support. After this, parents go with their children into the tutor groups to meet the teachers and ask any questions.

Soon after the start of their children's first term, parents are invited to a coffee evening with individual tutors and, some seven weeks after term starts, to individual consultation sessions with tutors. It is the school's policy not to arrange meetings with individual subject teachers, so the tutor coordinates reports from them.

The home–school reading initiative

The two members of the school's Special Needs Department have been running this project for three years. The project is for first-year pupils, and the parents of all the children who are identified as needing this help are invited to a meeting just before the end of the first half-term. The meeting begins with a short introduction to 'reading', which includes a reference to the volume of research underlining the vital role parents can play, and then the two teachers engage in role play. This is intended to show parents some of the ways in which they can share books with their children.

Parents are also given a small booklet of guidelines and a home–school book for teachers and parents to exchange written comments, in which pupils may write if they wish. An essential ingredient of the work is the visit made to the homes of all the children taking part, and these and the practicalities of the project, such as the days on which books will be exchanged, are explained.

A second meeting is held approximately six weeks later, and by this time all the parents will have been visited at home. This meeting is combined with a social gathering which is also attended by parents who took part in the project in previous years. The intention is that they will talk to the parents of first-year pupils about their experiences and about their children's subsequent progress.

The LEA's support for developing work with parents

The LEA had initiated a four-year project to promote the idea of 'parents as partners'. As well as inviting schools to submit requests for funding their work with parents, six advisory head-teachers were appointed. Each of these was attached to a district council area, as well as having a particular specialism, for example, 'Working with parents in the primary school'. As part of the LEA project, Overlea Comprehensive School was granted a substantial number of supply days to provide replacement teachers for those staff engaged in work with parents. The advisory headteacher attached to the school also offered to help in any appropriate way and provided school-based in-service training.

Summary, sample and method

The two strands of contact between home and school studied here, namely parents' involvement in relation to transition and the home–school reading initiative, came about because of the commitment of individual members of staff to certain aims. Both developments received extra impetus by means of re-sources from the local authority initiative.

In this school, one-quarter of the parents of first-year pupils (n = 22) were approached for interview and 21 agreed to take part. The four first-year tutors, the head of the first year and one of the deputy headteachers (who was acting headteacher at the time) were also interviewed. In addition, a variety of meetings for parents, including those concerned with transition, were attended.

Parents of the eight first-year children who had taken part in the shared reading project were approached for interview early in the term after the project, and seven agreed to take part. The head of the Special Needs Department was interviewed as was one of the first-year tutors who worked in her department and was involved in the project. Six of the pupils taking part were interviewed in school. The relevant meetings in school were attended.

The advisory headteacher was interviewed about her work in Overlea Comprehensive and the views of staff on provided support were obtained. Some in-service sessions run by the advisory headteacher were attended.

In addition to these 11 case studies, two other sources of information were included in the fieldwork.

The Parental Involvement Team in Stileborough – a team of advisory teachers who support schools to work with parents

This is an example of a permanent group of teachers, funded specifically to work with colleagues in schools and parents, to develop a variety of activities. This team was established five years ago in a small, urban authority which has a high proportion of Asian families and several densely populated housing-estates. The posts were initially funded for three years by an Urban Aid grant and are now financed by the education authority. It was originally intended that the team's work would span the three to 16 years age group, but many people assumed that it was confined to the early years sector (partly because the adviser involved has responsibility for early years education) and it is proving difficult to move up through the age range.

The project is directed by an adviser and the team consists of three advisory teachers, one of whom is designated as head of the team, and a nursery nurse. They work in schools across the authority to encourage parents to become involved as the educators of their own children; to promote a partnership between home and school; and to foster a welcoming atmosphere in schools. They undertake a variety of activities, including organizing parents' groups where aspects of the curriculum are explained and discussed, working in classrooms with parents and children, and home visiting, particularly where parents have been identified by schools as being in need of support. They also provide in-service training for teachers in the authority.

Method

The five members of staff connected with the team, including the adviser, were all interviewed.

The Parents' Consultative Group at Pendinge Comprehensive School

Pendinge is a comprehensive school with approximately 1,250 pupils, aged 11–18 years, and nearly 80 members of teaching staff. It is situated in a rural location, drawing pupils from a town and several outlying villages. The school serves a socially mixed, white catchment area.

The Parents' Consultative Group was established in the school when the recently appointed headteacher took up his post. He had organized similar gatherings in his previous school and was committed to this style of contact with parents. The headteacher believes that he should have information from as many sources as possible before making a decision and that schools are accountable to parents and must be open to them.

The group meets about once a month and, while it is hoped that at least two parents representing each year will be present, the meetings are open and the prospectus states that 'everyone is very welcome', and that 'It is a measure of how valuable these meetings are that many staff attend voluntarily'. Between 25 and 45 parents attend the meetings, which are designed as a forum for discussing and reviewing the work of each year group on the understanding that the headteacher will follow up any queries or concerns before the next meeting.

Issues raised range from homework and uniform to subject content and methods of recording pupil progress. Minutes of the meeting are published in the newsletter. Some of the meetings include a presentation by staff on some aspect of school life, for example, the teaching of English. A major concern of the group during the period of fieldwork was the procedure by which resources were allocated to the school by the LEA. There was correspondence to the authority on this and a senior member of staff from the education office came to address one meeting.

Method

Several group meetings and the Annual Parents' Meeting were attended during the course of this research. Discussing the form, content and aims of the group meetings with the head-teacher provided valuable insights into the potential of such forms of contact between home and school.

Appendix C
The Number of Respondents

	Number of respondents	
	Parents	Staff

Chapter 3   Parental involvement in the curriculum with their own children

	Parents	Staff
Going into school to work with their own children	116	27
Reading at home and at school	155	39
Activities to continue at home	155	34
Guidance from school for parents	155	34
Homework	79	26

Chapter 4   Meetings for parents

	Parents	Staff
Views on Annual Parents' Meetings	–	54

Chapter 5   Parental involvement at times of transition

	Parents	Staff
Views on transition	139	35

Chapter 6   Home visiting and other services

	Parents	Staff
Views on home visiting	181	73

Chapter 7   Day-to-day contacts between home and school

	Parents	Staff
Parents' Associations	161	41
Open/consultation sessions	148	45
Routine contact	117	50
Staff responsiveness to concerns	144	–
Improving contact	148	50
Written assessments	151	32
Open records	151	34
Written communication	131	–

	Number of respondents	
	Parents	Staff
Chapter 8 The organization of involvement		
Training to work with parents	–	58

References

ATKIN, J. and BASTIANI, J. (1984). *Preparing Teachers to Work with Parents: A Survey of Initial Training.* Nottingham: University of Nottingham School of Education.

BACHE, W. and NAUTA, M.J. (1979). *Homestart Follow-up Study: A Study of Longterm Impact of Homestart on Program Participants,* ED192 904 (available from the British Library).

BOEHM, A. (1970). *Boehm Test of Basic Concepts.* New York: Psychological Corporation.

BULLOCK REPORT (1975). *A Language for life.* London: HMSO.

CAMERON, R.J. (Ed) (1982). *Working Together: Portage in the UK.* Windsor: NFER-NELSON.

CENTRAL ADVISORY COUNCIL FOR EDUCATION (England) (Plowden) (1967). *Children and their Primary Schools,* Vol I: The Report; Vol II: Research and Surveys. London: HMSO.

CLEAVE, S., JOWETT, S. and BATE, M. (1982). *And So To School — A Study of Continuity from Pre-school to Infant School.* Windsor: NFER-NELSON.

COMMITTEE OF ENQUIRY INTO THE EDUCATION OF HANDICAPPED CHILDREN AND YOUNG PEOPLE (Warnock) (1978). *Special Educational Needs,* Cmnd 7212. London: HMSO.

DALE, N. (1986). 'Parents as partners — what does this mean to parents of children with special needs?', *Educational and Child Psychology,* **3**, 3, 191–200.

DALY, B., ADDINGTON, J., KERFOOT, S. and SIGSTON, A. (1985). *Portage: The Importance of Parents.* Windsor: NFER-NELSON.

DE'ATH, E. and PUGH, G. (Eds) (1986). *Working with Parents: A Training Resource Pack.* London: National Children's Bureau.

DEPARTMENT OF EDUCATION AND SCIENCE (Bullock) (1975). *A Language for Life.* London: HMSO.

DEPARTMENT OF EDUCATION AND SCIENCE (1989). *A Survey of Parent–School Liaison in Primary and Secondary Schools Serving Ethnically Diverse Areas within Three LEAs* (A Report by HM Inspectors). London: DES.

ELTON REPORT (1989). *Discipline in Schools*. London: HMSO.

GREAT BRITAIN. Statutes (1980). *Education Act 1980, Chapter 20*. London: HMSO.

GREAT BRITAIN. Statutes (1981). *Education Act 1981, Chapter 60*. London: HMSO.

GREAT BRITAIN. Statutes (1986). *Education Act (No. 2) 1986, Chapter 40*. London: HMSO.

GREAT BRITAIN. Statutes (1988). *Education Reform Act 1988, Chapter 40*. London: HMSO.

GREAT BRITAIN. DEPARTMENT OF EDUCATION AND SCIENCE/WELSH OFFICE (1989). *Discipline in Schools: Report of the Committee of Enquiry*, Chairman Lord Elton. London: HMSO.

JOHNSON, D. and RANSOM, E. (1983). *Family and the School*. London: HMSO.

JOWETT, S. (1989). 'Coping with change – children's experiences of transitions to new educational environments', *Maladjustment and Therapeutic Education*, **7**, 2, 92–98.

JOWETT, S. and BAGINSKY, M. (1988). 'Parents and education – a survey of their involvement and a discussion of some issues', *Educational Research*, **30**, 1, 36–45.

KATZ, L. (1982). 'Contemporary perspectives on the roles of mothers and teachers', *Australian Journal of Early Childhood*, **7**, 1, 4–15.

LAZAR, I. and DARLINGTON, R. (1982). *Lasting Effects of Early Education: A Report from the Consortium for Longitudinal Studies*, Monographs of the Society for Research in Child Development, Serial no. 195, 47.

MITTLER, P. and MITTLER, H. (1982). *Partnership with Parents*. Stratford-upon-Avon: National Council for Special Education.

MORTIMORE, P., SAMMONS, P., STOLL, L., LEWIS, D. and ECOB, R. (1988). *School Matters – The Junior Years*. Taunton: Open Books.

PETCH, A. (1986). 'Parental choice at entry to primary school', *Research Papers in Education*, **1**, 1, 26–47.

PLOWDEN REPORT. GREAT BRITAIN. DEPARTMENT OF EDUCATION AND SCIENCE. CENTRAL ADVISORY COUNCIL FOR EDUCATION (ENGLAND) (1967). *Children and their Primary Schools*. London: HMSO.

PUGH, G., APLIN, G., DE'ATH, E. and MOXON, M. (1987a). *Partnership in Action: Working with Parents in Pre-school Centres*, Vol. 1. London: National Children's Bureau.

PUGH, G. et al. (1987b). *Partnership in Action: Working with Parents in Pre-school Centres*, Vol. 2. London: National Children's Bureau.

STILLMAN, A. and MAYCHELL, K. (1986). *Choosing Schools: Parents, LEAs and the 1980 Education Act*. Windsor: NFER-NELSON.

TIZARD, B. and HUGHES, M. (1984). *Young Children Learning*. London: Fontana.

TIZARD, B., BLATCHFORD, P., BURKE, J., FARQUHAR, C. and PLEWIS, I. (1988). *Young Children at School in the Inner City*. London: Lawrence Erlbaum.

TIZARD, B., MORTIMORE, J. and BURCHELL, B. (1981). *Involving Parents in Nursery and Infant School*. London: Grant McIntyre.

TIZARD, J., SCHOFIELD, W. N. and HEWISON, J. (1982). 'Symposium: Reading – collaboration between teachers and parents in assisting children's reading', *British Journal of Educational Psychology*, **52**, 1, 1–15.

TOPPING, K. (1985). 'An introduction to paired reading'. In: TOPPING, K. and WOLFENDALE, S. (Eds) *Parental Involvement in Children's Reading*. London: Croom Helm, 109–114.

WARNOCK REPORT. COMMITTEE OF ENQUIRY INTO THE EDUCATION OF HANDICAPPED CHILDREN AND YOUNG PEOPLE (1978). *Special Educational Needs*. London: HMSO.

WATT, J. (1988). 'From nursery school to primary school – a symbolic transition', *OMEP (World Organisation for Early Childhood Education) UPDATE*, 26.

WEIKART, D. (1971). *The Cognitively Orientated Curriculum*. Washington, DC: National Association for the Education of Young Children.

WIDLAKE, P. and MACLEOD, F. (1984). *Raising Standards. Parental Involvement Programmes and the Language Performance of Children*. Coventry: Community Education Development Centre.

WINKLEY, D. (1985). 'The school's view of parents'. In: CULLINGFORD, C. (Ed) *Parents, Teachers and Schools*. London: Robert Royce.

WOODS, P. (1984). *Parents and School: A Report for Discussion on Views between Parents and Secondary Schools in Wales*. London: School Curriculum Development Committee.

THE NFER RESEARCH LIBRARY

Titles available in the NFER Research Library

	HARDBACK	SOFTBACK
TITLE	*ISBN*	*ISBN*
Joining Forces: a study of links between special and ordinary schools (Jowett, Hegarty, Moses)	0 7005 1179 2	0 7005 1162 8
Supporting Ordinary Schools; LEA initiatives (Moses, Hegarty, Jowett)	0 7005 1177 6	0 7005 1163 6
Developing Expertise: INSET for special educational needs (Moses and Hegarty (Eds))	0 7005 1178 4	0 7005 1164 4
Graduated Tests in Mathematics: a study of lower attaining pupils in secondary schools (Foxman, Ruddock, Thorpe)	0 7005 0867 8	0 7005 0868 6
Mathematics Coordination: a study of practice in primary and middle schools (Stow with Foxman)	0 7005 0873 2	0 7005 0874 0
A Sound Start: the schools' instrumental music service (Cleave and Dust)	0 7005 0871 6	0 7005 0872 4
Course Teams – the Way Forward in FE? (Tansley)	0 7005 0869 4	0 7005 0870 8
The LEA Adviser – a Changing Role (Stillman, Grant)	0 7005 0875 9	0 7005 0876 7
Languages for a Change: diversifying foreign language provision in schools (Rees)	0 7005 1202 0	0 7005 1203 9
The Time to Manage? department and faculty heads at work (Earley and Fletcher-Campbell)	0 7005 1233 0	0 7005 1234 9

	HARDBACK	SOFTBACK
GCSE in Practice: managing assessment innovation (Grant)	0 7005 1239 X	0 7005 1240 3
Moving into the Mainstream: LEA provision for bilingual pupils (Bourne):	0 7005 1235 7	0 7005 1236 5
Beyond Vision: training for work with visually impaired people (Maychell and Smart)	0 7005 1245 4	0 7005 1246 2
Records of Achievement in the Marketplace (Ashforth)	0 7005 1251 9	0 7005 1250 0

For further information contact the Customer Support Department, NFER-NELSON, Darville House, 2 Oxford Road East, Windsor, Berks SL4 1DF, England. Tel: (0753) 858961   Telex 937400 ONECOM G Ref. 24966001